Messaging Made Agile

Strategy First, AI Second

The Leader's Guide to Precision Communication

Jorma Manninen

BUSINESS MADE AGILE
WWW.BUSINESSMADEAGILE.COM

Published by Business Made Agile Oy (Ltd.)
Pori, Finland

Book version 1.0 (First Printing, January 2026)
Book design: Author.
Cover design: Author.

Printed in the United States of America.

ISBN 978-952-65893-0-5 (softcover)
ISBN 978-952-65893-1-2 (hardcover)
ISBN 978-952-65893-2-9 (EPUB)
ISBN 978-952-65893-3-6 (PDF)

BUSINESS MADE AGILE

Messaging Made Agile

Dedicated to the unknown leaders who navigate uncertainty with courage and lead others with empathy and authority.

The Silent Struggle

You see it in reports, you hear it in meetings, and you smell it in the air. Your strategies are approved but not executed.

You talk to your staff, you watch them listen, and you feel it in your guts. Your messages are heard but not accepted.

You watch good ideas lose, you watch bad ideas win, and you know why. Bad writing gets good ideas rejected, but good writing gets even bad ideas accepted.

So, bad writing is the problem, but AI is not the solution. It can write, but it can't think. You think. You are the strategist. AI is your assistant.

Strategy First, AI Second

FOREWORD

In the decades I have spent teaching and consulting on the art of strategic messaging, I have consistently argued with one point: communication is not an administrative chore; it is a business lever. Whether in the lecture halls of Alabama or the executive classrooms of the Aalto EMBA in Helsinki, my goal has been to move leaders away from "writing" and toward "strategic thinking."

When Jorma Manninen sat in my classroom over a decade ago, it was clear he understood this distinction. He didn't just want to know how to phrase a sentence; he wanted to know how to move a boardroom. He understood that every message carries a "Bottom-Line" responsibility.

Since then, the world has changed. In November 2022, the introduction of Generative AI created a paradox for the modern leader. On one hand, we have gained unprecedented speed. On the other, we are witnessing the birth of a new organizational disease that Jorma aptly calls "Workslop," the production of grammatically perfect but strategically hollow noise that drains leadership capacity and confuses the mission.

In Messaging Made Agile, Jorma does something that few other authors in the AI space have managed: he restores the leader to the center of the process.

He argues—correctly—that while AI is a powerful "jet engine," it is a mindless one. Without a human Pilot to define the Commander's Intent, the machine simply accelerates the drift. By introducing the Traffic Light Model and the Core AI Workflow, Jorma has created a modern "Flight Manual" that takes the strategic messaging principles I have long championed and applies them to the high velocity demands of 2026.

This book is a timely warning against the "Passenger Mindset." It is a call for executives to reclaim the 1,200 hours currently lost to the digital void. Jorma's "Strategy First, AI Second" approach is the only way to ensure that in an age of machine-generated volume, human clarity remains the ultimate competitive advantage.

For any leader who feels they are losing their voice to the machine, or their time to the inbox, this book is your return to the cockpit. Take the controls.

Dr. Ronald E. Dulek
John R. Miller Professor of Management
The University of Alabama

PREFACE

There is a storm coming. It is a storm of noise.

If you work over 60 hours a week on average, you are most likely a business owner, CEO, or senior executive. And you spend 1,200 hours a year on non-face-to-face interactions, reading reports, emails, and other messages that fail to communicate the main point, the bottom line.

Miscommunication is the noise. Bad writing is the villain that causes miscommunication, waste of time, and a loss of productivity valued at over $12,000 a year per employee.

For thirty years, I have navigated the complexities of international business, not just as an observer, but as a practitioner. My journey has taken me from Export Sales and Business Development to the boardroom, serving as a Project Manager, Key Account Manager, Business Unit Manager, Post-Merger Integration Program Manager, Chief Marketing Officer, and eventually as a CEO and Chairman.

I have led Joint Ventures, capital projects, presided over the Thai-Finnish Chamber of Commerce, and served on boards across Europe and Southeast Asia. In each of these roles, I felt the weight of the decisions on the table.

In those three decades, I learned one timeless truth: Brilliant strategies don't fail because they are flawed; they fail because they are communicated poorly. I have seen millions of dollars evaporate in the gap between what a leader meant and what the team understood.

For decades, the solution to this problem was slow, deliberate training. We taught leaders to pause, to think, and to write with care. As Mark Twain famously said, "I didn't have time to write a short letter, so I wrote a long one instead."

Then, everything changed. ChatGPT was released on November 30, 2022. It marked the arrival of Generative AI into mainstream public consciousness. Gen AI has fundamentally altered the landscape of leadership. Suddenly, the friction of writing vanished. We can now generate emails, reports, and strategies at the speed of light. But this new speed has created a new and dangerous paradox: we are communicating faster than ever, but we are connecting less than ever.

As a leader, you feel this. You see the inbox filling up with "synthetic text", professional, polite, and completely empty. You feel the pressure to move faster, to hand your voice over to the machine, and to trade your authenticity for efficiency.

I know this temptation because I have felt it myself. In early 2023, just weeks after ChatGPT entered the world, I established my consulting firm to help companies navigate this reality. I dove headfirst into new technology. I started using AI to rewrite my writing and repurpose content. The speed was intoxicating. It was remarkably easy to become "addicted" to efficiency, watching the machine generate in seconds what used to take me hours. But I quickly realized the trap: I was generating more, but I was leading less.

This book provides a path to reclaim your leadership from the noise. It is not a guide on how to use AI to do more; it is a guide on how to use AI to write better and work faster.

It is built on a framework I call ***Strategy First, AI Second*** This playbook allows you to harness the unlimited speed of these new tools without sacrificing the clarity, empathy, and authority that define true leadership.

The cost of ignoring this shift is absolute. Analysts from Gartner to McKinsey predict that by 2030, AI will touch nearly every aspect of knowledge work. They forecast that up to 80% of routine project management tasks will be eliminated by AI, and that successful organizations won't just have the best technology; they will collaborate best with AI.

I predict that by 2030, the "Average" leader will be obsolete. The middle ground, where leaders simply pass information from one layer to another, will be automated. The leaders who survive and thrive will be the ones who can do what the machine cannot: define the vision, inject empathy, and command the strategy.

By mastering the craft of precision communication, you do more than save your own time. You become a coach for your team. You lift others out of the fog of bad writing. And your reward is an organization that runs on clear, concise, and high-impact messages. As you stand on the edge of this new era, you must answer one question:

Are you the Leader, or do you allow machines take over?

My answer is simple: You are the Leader, the Strategist, and AI is your Assistant, the Writer. And this book is your guide to precision communication. It is time to be the Leader.

Turn the page. Let's get to work.

Jorma Manninen

CONTENTS

CONTENTS

Messaging Made Agile

Strategy First, AI Second

INTRODUCTION

Do you work 60+ hours a week? If so, you are likely a CEO or senior executive on the fast track. But here is the diagnostic question that matters: How many of those hours are spent leading, and how many are lost to the "digital void"?

As Michael Porter and Nitin Nohria noted in Harvard Business Review, *"Time is the scarcest resource leaders have. Where they allocate it matters a lot."* A landmark HBS CEO Time Study found that CEOs spend 39% of their time on non-face-to-face interactions. That is 24 hours a week, **1,200 hours a year,** consumed by the relentless demands of digital messages.

This isn't just a professional burden; it is a profound strategic leak. When the boardroom becomes a "Formula 1 pit stop" and your inbox becomes a primary workplace, you aren't steering the ship, you're bailing water. Financially, miscommunication is a silent killer, draining an estimated **$12,506 per employee annually** in lost productivity. For a mid-sized enterprise, which is a multi-million-dollar tax on existence.

It's also a personal cost. Just like the boardroom, your bedroom at home becomes a "pit stop" rather than a place for recovery.

The Stakes: From Memos to Market Crash

Bad writing is not a "soft skill" issue; it is an enterprise-level risk. In high-stakes scenarios, tone-deaf language triggers catastrophic consequences.

United Airlines Crisis (2017). After a passenger was violently removed from a flight, CEO Oscar Munoz issued a memo describing the victim as "disruptive and belligerent." By prioritizing procedural compliance over human empathy, the message fueled a global backlash that erased nearly $1 billion in market value in a single day.

"Nut Rage" Scandal (2014). When a Korean Air executive's tantrum over macadamia nuts went viral, the airline's generic, PR-scrubbed apologies were perceived as insincere "stunts." The resulting public outrage didn't just hurt the brand; it led to criminal charges and the resignation of the Chairman's daughter and a 12-month prison sentence.

In both cases, the failure wasn't in the *intent*, it was in the *execution* of the message.

The Authority: Escaping the Trap of Synthetic Leadership

In early 2023, I dove headfirst into Generative AI. The speed was intoxicating. It was easy to become "addicted" to efficiency, watching machines generate in seconds what used to take me hours. But I quickly realized the trap: I was generating more, but I was leading less. My authenticity was being traded for volume. I was producing "synthetic text" i.e., words that were grammatically perfect but strategically hollow.

This realization led me to establish my consulting firm, **Business Made Agile**, to help companies navigate this new reality. With 30 years of international business experience, from export sales to the boardroom, I have seen millions evaporate in the gap between what a leader meant and what people understood. AI was making that gap wider, not narrower.

The Big Idea: Strategy First, AI Second

I authored this book to give you a path to harness machine speed without sacrificing human authority. Generative AI is a magic wand that can also be an accelerant for noise. **AI is brilliant at generating words without making a point.** Prompting an AI without a message strategy is like handing an F1 car to a novice driver: you'll reach the wall faster than ever before.

To thrive, you must adopt the right mindset: ***Strategy First, AI Second*** This is built on two foundational pillars:

- **The Agile Message Strategy:** Your human-led blueprint for defining Commander's Intent, predicting reactions, and selecting the perfect structural pattern (Direct, Hybrid, or Indirect).
- **The Core AI Workflow:** Your machine-accelerated engine—the Prompt - Refine - Personalize cycle—to generate clarity at scale while protecting your authentic voice.

The 5 Principles of Precision Communication

Precision is the strategic combination of absolute clarity, active curiosity, and radical empathy. To move from theory to execution, we use the following five dials to calibrate every message for maximum precision:

- **Prioritize Responsiveness:** Remove organizational friction by responding in minutes rather than days. In an agile environment, velocity is a strategic advantage that builds trust.
- **Cultivate Curiosity:** Spend 80% of your time asking insightful questions rather than dominating the narrative. True authority comes from understanding the landscape before attempting to command it.

- **Deliver Absolute Value:** Ensure every message is engineered to help the recipient succeed (WIIFM). Eliminate the "ego-driven" update and replace it with tangible utility.
- **Demand Crystalline Clarity:** Use simple, punchy language that anyone in the organization can understand. Refuse to hide behind the fog of corporate jargon or complex sentence structures.
- **Engineer for Impact:** Aim for a "Wow" through measurable utility. If a message does not clarify a path or solve a problem, it is merely adding to the noise.

To lead effectively in the AI era, you must treat these five principles as high-performance "dials" for every message you send.

The 4 Values of the Agile Communicator

To maintain speed without losing impact, you must:

- **Prioritize Message Outcomes over Comprehensive Prose:** Focus exclusively on tangible results and absolute clarity. Value the outcome produced by the message over the length or documentation of the prose.
- **Champion Audience Collaboration over One-Way Broadcasting:** Move away from "fire and forget" emails. Establish reader-centric feedback loops that turn communication into a collaborative dialogue.
- **Assert Human Strategy over Automated Tools:** Command AI as a powerful strategic accelerator but don't allow it to function as a replacement for human judgment, empathy, and accountability.
- **Respond to Feedback over Following a Script:** Use real-time data and audience sentiment to adapt your message dynamically. Be prepared to pivot your approach as the situation unfolds rather than adhering to a rigid plan.

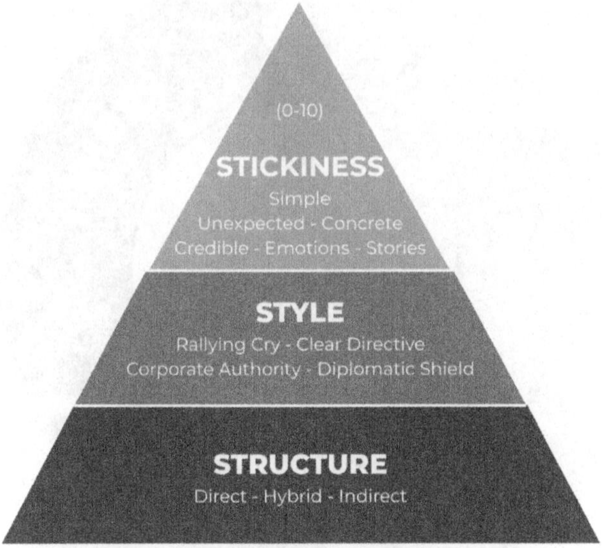

THE AGILE MESSAGE STRATEGY

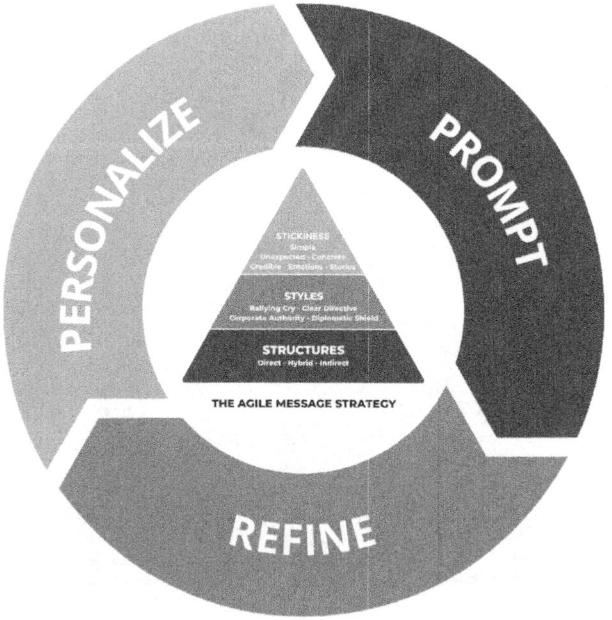

THE CORE AI WORKFLOW

The Scope: Who is This Book For?

This book is for CEOs, senior executives, and top-tier managers responsible for the strategy and productivity of complex organizations. To understand where your message fits, we use The Agile Communicator's Matrix and The Agile Messenger's Matrix.

The Agile Communicator's Matrix

Maps communication across quadrants (Strategic vs. Tactical). Use this to ensure your high-level goals don't get lost in low-level channels.

- **Strategic Communication:** Building long-term brands, culture, and vision.
- **Strategic Messaging:** Guiding behavior toward specific outcomes (The "What" and "So What?").
- **Tactical Communication:** The systems and channels used for delivery.
- **Tactical Messaging:** Immediate, actionable content (The "Now What?").

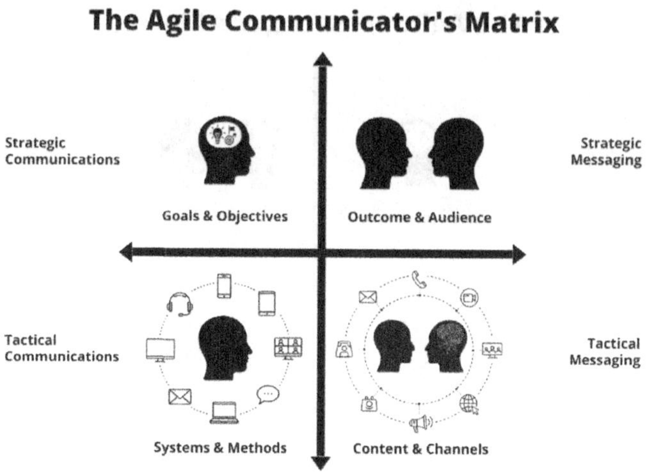

The Agile Messenger's Matrix

Relates messaging to decision-making (Proactive vs. Reactive). Use this to move from reactive crisis-fighting to proactive brand-building.

- **Strategic Proactive:** Carefully planned campaigns designed to build perception and relationships.
- **Tactical Proactive:** Scheduled, action-oriented messages that drive planned results.
- **Strategic Reactive:** High-stakes responses to unplanned events that must align with long-term values.
- **Tactical Reactive:** Immediate responses to day-to-day operational issues.

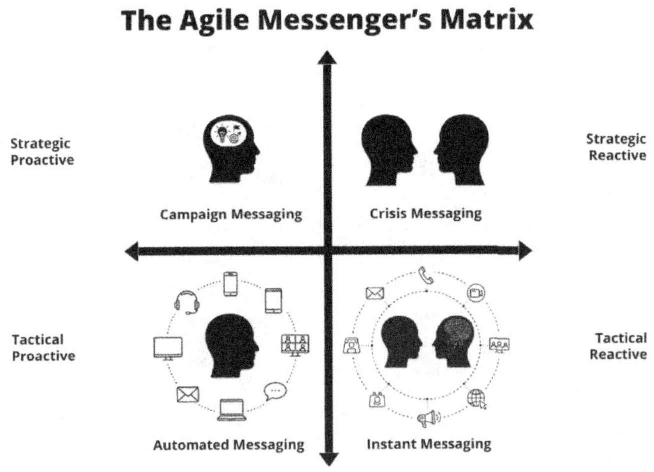

The Agile Messenger's Roadmap

Reclaiming your time and mastering precision communication happens in three distinct stages:

- **Step 1: Master the Strategic Foundation.** Learn to think like an analyst before you write like a leader. You will define your Commander's Intent, the **Agile Message Strategy**, and select the right message structure (Direct, Hybrid, or Indirect) before typing a single word.
- **Step 2: Craft the Message.** You will learn to select the right Style, apply the science of Stickiness, and use the StoryBrand framework to ensure your ideas aren't just read but remembered and accepted.
- **Step 3: Command Your AI Assistant.** Implement the **Core AI Workflow** to move from being a passive writer to a "Pilot" who commands AI to generate crystalline clarity at scale without sacrificing your authentic authority.

In an age of synthetic text, your authenticity, being true to your values and voice, is your ultimate competitive advantage. Before you move to Part I, ask yourself: Are you the Pilot-in-Command in the cockpit or just a passenger in the cabin? Has your AI Copilot already seized command and control?"

It is time to get back to the cockpit and take the controls.

.

Messaging Made Agile

Strategy First, AI Second

Part I: The Strategic Foundation

Jorma Manninen

BUSINESS MADE AGILE

WWW.BUSINESSMADEAGILE.COM

PART I EXECUTIVE SUMMARY: THE ANALYST'S TOOLKIT

THE BOTTOM LINE

Precision communication is not a writing skill; it is a strategic discipline. Before you touch a keyboard or a chatbot, you must function as an Analyst.

Part I provides the blueprint for "Step Zero", **the human-led strategy** that ensures you never accelerate a bad idea with AI.

KEY TAKEAWAYS

The Unbreakable Rule: Audience Over Author Stop writing for yourself! Every message must answer three questions for the reader instantly:

- **What?** (The Facts)
- **So What?** (The Relevance)
- **Now What?** (The Action)

The Commander's Intent Define the Statement of the End State before you write. If your team doesn't know the ultimate "What" and "Why," they cannot adapt when the plan changes.

The Traffic Light Structures Match your message organization to the audience's emotional state:

- **Green Light (Direct):** Main point first. Use for 90% of business messages.
- **Yellow Light (Hybrid):** Build the case before the "ask." Use for organizing messages for skeptical audiences.
- **Red Light (Indirect):** Rationale first, bad news second. Use for organizing messages for disappointed external audiences.

The Role-Based Workflow Kills writer's block by separating concerns into five distinct professional hats: Leader, Analyst, Researcher, Writer, and Editor.

Decision-Making Under Pressure (OODA) Use the Observe-Orient-Decide-Act loop to respond to crises in 90 seconds rather than 10 minutes.

THE STRATEGY FIRST CHECKLIST

- Do I have a clear Statement of the End State, the Desired Outcome?
- Have I analyzed and predicted the audience's emotional reaction?
- Have I selected the message structure based on that reaction?
- Am I prepared to function as a Pilot, not a Passenger?

CHAPTER 1: INTRODUCTION TO PART I

The Strategic Foundation

This section establishes the core of the "Strategy First, AI Second" framework. But before you can command an AI Assistant to write for you, you must first master the art of thinking for yourself. A clear message requires a clear strategy. If your strategy is fuzzy, your AI Assistant will simply accelerate your confusion.

Part I is your "Analyst's Toolkit." It is designed to transform you from a reactive writer into a proactive strategist. By the end of this section, you will not just know about strategic messaging; you will have a proven system for executing it.

Your Mission

In the following chapters, you will move beyond the basics of "writing" and learn the specific, high-level skills of the **Agile Analyst:**

You will master the "Unbreakable Rule" (Chapter 2) You will learn to flip the script on traditional business writing. You will stop writing for yourself and start writing entirely for your reader, using **Emotional Intelligence** to predict their reactions and **Audience Analysis** to ensure your message lands.

You will master the "Strategy Brief" (Chapters 3) You will learn to define your **Commander's Intent**, the specific, measurable, desired outcome you want to produce, before you type a single word. You will learn to select the right Communication Channels, define success metrics, and decide your **Transparency Strategy** for AI usage.

You will master the "Message Structure" (Chapter 4) You will stop guessing how to organize your thoughts. You will learn to select the perfect **Structure** (Direct, Hybrid, or Indirect) based on your audience's emotional state, ensuring your message is not just read, but accepted.

You will master the "Agile Workflow" (Chapter 5) You will learn to stop trying to do everything at once. You will adopt a professional, role-based workflow **(Leader, Analyst, Researcher, Writer, Editor)** that kills writer's block and prepares you for AI integration.

You will master Decision-Making Under Pressure (Chapter 6) You will learn to apply the **OODA Loop** (Observe, Orient, Decide, Act) to crisis communication, giving you the speed and agility to lead when the stakes are highest.

This is the strategic foundation. Once you have mastered these human-led strategies, you will be ready to learn how to craft your messages with the right style and how to make your messages stick in Part II.

Let's begin with the one rule you must never break.

CHAPTER 2: THE ONE UNBREAKABLE RULE IN BUSINESS WRITING

In business writing, a strange transformation happens. When we are readers, we are ruthless. We scan, we judge, and we ignore anything that doesn't immediately solve our problem. But when we sit down to write, we become irrational. We obsess over what we want to say, how smart we sound, and what we need to get off our chest. This disconnect is the single greatest cause of communication failure.

The cure is simple, but difficult to execute. It is the one unbreakable rule in business writing:

It is not about you. It is about the reader.

To be an effective leader, you must stop writing to validate your own ideas and start writing to serve your audience. You must move from an "author-centric" mindset to an "audience-centric" strategy. This chapter gives you the tools to make that shift.

The Four Domains of Emotional Intelligence

This "Reader-First, Writer Second" mindset is a practical application of Emotional Intelligence (EI). It is the ability to predict, with high accuracy, how your message will land and how your audience will react to it before you send it. This translates into four strategic EI domains for Agile Communicators:

1. Self-Awareness (The Check-In) This is your internal audit. Before you write, ask: *Am I writing to inform, or am I writing to vent?* An Agile Analyst recognizes when their own frustration is leaking into the draft and potentially sabotaging the message. Ask yourself: "Should I write or reply to this message, or should someone else do it?"

2. Self-Management (The Tone Control) This is your ability to separate your feelings from your keyboard. Even when you are stressed or angry, you must choose a tone that is professional and constructive. It is the discipline to write what is *effective*, not just what feels satisfying in the moment. After you have written your message ask yourself once more: "Should I send the message or not? Write your messages first and save them as drafts. Read them aloud before you send them.

3. Social Awareness (The Prediction Engine) This is the core skill of the Analyst. It goes beyond simple empathy; it is the strategic ability to predict your audience's emotional reaction. *Will this make them defensive? Will they be skeptical?* Accurate prediction allows you to choose the right message structure to mitigate risk.

4. Relationship Management (The Trust Builder) This is the long-term play. Every message you send either builds trust or erodes it. An Agile Analyst uses communication to resolve conflict, coach performance, and inspire action, ensuring that the "relationship capital" is always growing.

When your target audience receives your message, they think:

- **What do you want from me?** What's the Bottom Line?
- **So, what's in it for me?** Why should I care?
- **Now what should I do?** What do I do next?

If your message cannot answer these questions instantly, it has failed.

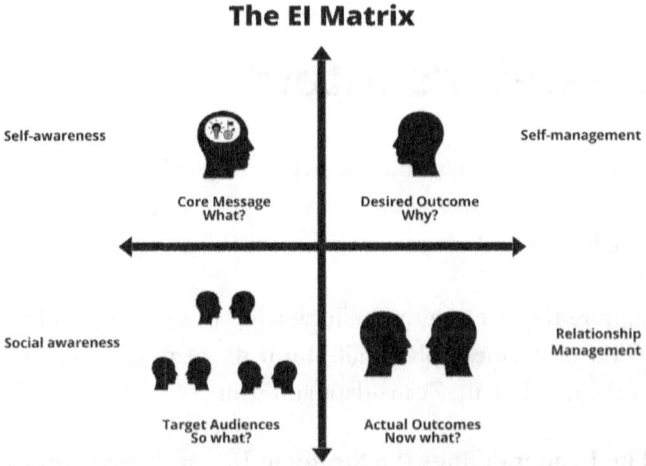

The EI Matrix isn't just a soft-skill tool; it's a financial safeguard. By mastering Social Awareness and Self-Management, you prevent the 'Synthetic Leadership' lapses that crashed United's stock price. Every tone-deaf memo is a withdrawal from your company's market value; Precision Communication ensures you're making deposits instead.

Agile Communicator's Razor

This is the Agile Communicator's razor. It forces you to strip away all fluff and focus purely on utility.

- **What? (The Facts)** This is the objective reality. What happened? What is the data? For example: "Our website was down for two hours today."
- **So What? (The Relevance)** This is the interpretation. Why does this matter to the reader? What is the impact? For example: "This cost us $15,000 in lost sales and triggered 50 support tickets."
- **Now What? (The Action)** This is the next step. What is the plan? For example: "We are installing a backup server tonight to ensure this never happens again."

By forcing every message through this filter, you ensure it is impossible to be misunderstood.

Commander's Intent

The first question an Analyst must answer is "Why?"

Most writers stop at a weak "activity" goal: I am writing to inform the team. An Agile Leader defines a specific "action" goal: I am writing to get the budget approved.

To capture this, we use the military concept of Commander's Intent. In the fog of war or business, plans fail. But if the team understands the Intent, the goal of the mission, they can adapt and win.

- **The Leader defines the Strategic Intent. (The Purpose):** W*hy?* This is the larger objective you are trying to achieve, for example: "The final desired outcome is that the client views us as a strategic partner, not just a vendor."
- **The Leader defines the Desired Outcome (The Action):** What? This is the specific, tangible action you want your reader to take. It is the Statement of the End State of the Commander's Intent.

This clarity is what separates a leader from a manager. If your desired outcome is just *to get a client to renew,* you might focus on discounts. If your Strategic Intent is *to make this client a long-term strategic partner,* you'll focus on demonstrating future value and building trust. Before you write, define both.

Audience Analysis Checklist

The second step of the Analyst's work is to diagnose the target audience.

Predicted Impact

- [ ] Positive
- [ ] Negative,
- [ ] Non-sensitive

Trust Level

- [ ] High
- [ ] Average
- [ ] Low

Power Position

- [ ] Upward, targeting superiors
- [ ] Parallel, targeting peers.
- [ ] Downward, targeting subordinates.

Business Context

- [ ] Internal, targeting superiors, peers, or subordinates.
- [ ] External, targeting customers, partners, suppliers, or other stakeholders.

Relationship

- [ ] Customer
- [ ] Business Partner
- [ ] Supplier
- [ ] Government

Cultural Context

- [ ] Low Context: Use Direct structure, Bottom Line Up First
- [ ] High Context: Use Indirect structure, Bottom Line Down Last

Payoff

By answering these questions, you answer reader's question: What's in it for me? (WIIFM). You bridge the gap between your Commander's Intent and their reality. This is the secret to persuasion. It is not about writing better sentences; it is about solving the reader's problem.

Now that you have analyzed your audience and defined your intent, you are ready for the next step and make three final, high-level strategic decisions that "bookend" your entire communication.

CHAPTER 3: THE FINAL STRATEGY LAYERS

In Chapter 2, you built the core of your Agile Message Strategy by answering the three foundational questions: What is your Strategic Intent? Why are your writing? Who is your target audience? Why do they care?

Now you have a clear purpose, a deep understanding of your audience, and a compelling angle.

But before you can move on to choosing a Message Type, you must make three final, high-level strategic decisions that "bookend" your entire communication.

- **Communication Channels** How will the message be delivered?
- **Measurement Criteria** How will you know if you succeeded?
- **Transparency Strategy** How will you manage authenticity?

Answering these questions completes your "Agile Message Strategy" and ensures your message is not just a wild guess, but a complete, measurable plan.

Communication Channels

Most leaders use email for all messages by default. This is a mistake. The medium is part of the message. Sending a sensitive critique as an SMS is a leadership failure; announcing a major win via a buried intranet post is a missed opportunity.

To be an Agile Communicator, you must stop choosing channels based on convenience and start choosing them based on function.

The Agile Channel Selector

Strategic Intent	Channels
Evidence & Record	Emails: Gmail, MS Outlook, Yahoo Mail, Apple Mail, Zoho Mail, etc.
Speed & Operation	Instant Messages: WhatsApp, WeChat, Facebook Messenger, Telegram, Snapchat, Discord, Line, MS Teams, Slack, etc.
Nuance & Consensus	Meetings: In-person / online, Zoom, MS Teams, Google Meet, Webex, etc.
Broadcast & Culture	Intranet / videos: Simpplr, Workvivo, Jostle, Unily, Slack, MS Teams, Google Workspace, etc.
Urgent Attention	SMS / phone calls / push notifications, AlertMedia, Everbridge, CodeRED, etc.
Public Engagement & Brand	Social media: LinkedIn, X, Facebook, Instagram, Pinterest, TikTok
Targeted Promotion	Ads: LinkedIn Ads, Google Ads, Facebook Ads, Paid Media, etc.

CEO Pro Tip

While you must set the Strategic Intent, you don't always need to be the one picking channel. Delegate Tactical Communication, the choice of medium, to your Analysts and Writers. Your job is to define the 'Commander's Intent'; their job is to use the Channel Selector to ensure that intent reaches the target without distortion.

Here are reasons why the channels work for strategic intents:

- **Emails** create a searchable, time-to-stamped "paper trail." Ideal for formalizing decisions, contracts, and directives that may need to be referenced later.
- **Instant messages** are best for rapid coordination, quick questions, and non-sensitive updates. Reduces friction and email clutter. Rule: Never use instant messages for criticism or sensitive feedback.
- **Meetings / online meetings** are best for sensitive feedback, complex brainstorming, or aligning a team on a controversial topic. Tone, body language, and immediate feedback are critical here.
- **Intranet / videos** are best for one-to-many announcements where tone matters. Helps create and reinforce company culture and ensure consistent messaging across the organization.
- **SMS / phone calls / push notifications** are best for true emergencies that require immediate action and cannot wait for an email or IM check. Use sparingly to respect boundaries.
- **Social media** is best for external communication to build brand authority, engage with customers, and attract talent. It is public, performative, and interactive.
- **Ads** are best for reaching specific external audiences with a tailored persuasive message to drive specific action (click, buy, sign up).

The Strategic Rules for Channel Selection

- **The "No-Surprise" Rule:** Never deliver bad news like firing or budget cuts via a text-based channel such as Email, SMS, or Slack. Always use a high-bandwidth channel such as in-person meeting or online meeting. If you call first, then you can send written confirmation.

- **The "Deep Work" Rule:** Respect your team's focus. Default to asynchronous channels like Email or Slack for *non-urgent* items so they can respond when they are ready. Use synchronous channels like phone calls or meetings only when *urgent* real-time interaction is necessary.
- **The "One Source of Truth" Rule:** For operational tasks, designate one channel as the official record. For example: "All design feedback must go in Figma comments, not Slack" or "All final decisions must be emailed". This prevents information fragmentation.

The Agile Channel Selector matrix gives you a complete "menu" of options, ensuring you always pick the right tool for the job based on your specific strategic intent. The Golden Rule of Agile Channels:

Never use a synchronous channel for an asynchronous task.

Respect your team's work time: If it can be read, write it. If it must be discussed, schedule it.

Success Measurement

This is the second critical question, and it's the one that turns your communication from an activity into a strategy.

The most common mistake in communication planning is confusing the means with the end. A "communications goal", for example, "to send an email" is not a business outcome. Communication is the tool you use to achieve a real, observable result.

As communications expert David Grossman argues, your "desired outcome" must be a tangible change in business performance. "If you don't know where you're going, any road will get you there."

You can measure success on two levels:

- Business Outcomes
- Secondary Outcomes

Business Outcomes: The Business Metrics

This is the measurable, observable result. This should be your primary criteria.

- **The Approval:** "Did I get the “yes” on the budget?"
- **The Adoption:** "Did 100% of the team switch to the new software?"
- **The Reduction:** "Did customer support tickets drop by 10%?"

Secondary Outcomes: The Agile Metrics

Sometimes, the goal is speed or relationship capital.

- **Speed to Execution:** "How long between my email and the team taking action?" This is the ultimate agile metric. A clear message reduces this lag to zero.
- **Sentiment:** "Did the client's tone shift from hostile to collaborative in their reply?"

Transparency Strategy

As we will discuss in detail in Chapter 18, the use of AI introduces a new strategic layer: **Authenticity.**

Should you tell your team you used AI?

- **Yes:** If you are building a process, for example: "I used AI to summarize these meeting notes".
- **No:** If you are building a relationship, for example: "I used AI to write this condolence note"

The Leader's Rule of Thumb

- If the message builds trust, write it yourself or personalize it heavily.
- If the message builds process, let AI help and be transparent about it.

Why this matters now: Authenticity is currency. If your team suspects you are automating your empathy, you lose trust. If they suspect you are hiding your tools, you lose credibility. Deciding your transparency level before you write ensures you don't accidentally send a robotic message that damages your reputation.

The Agile Message Strategy Brief

By answering the questions in Chapters 2 and 3, you have completed your "Step Zero." You now have a complete strategy.

Before you write or prompt your AI, fill out this one-page brief. This is your roadmap.

The Agile Message Strategy Brief

Commander's Intent (Why? & What?)

- Strategic Intent
- Desired Outcome

Target Audience (Who?)

- Who are they?
- Emotional State
- WIIFM

The Plan (How?)

- Communication Channels
- Success Measurement Criteria
- Transparency Strategy

You are now ready to execute. In the next chapter, we will take this brief and choose the perfect Message Structure to deliver it.

CHAPTER 4: THE MESSAGE STRUCTURE

In Chapter 3, we introduced the communication channels and measurement criteria for success as well as transparency strategy for AI. This chapter is focused on the core of the Agile Message Strategy: **The Structure.**

A clear, logically structured message commands attention and drives action. A brilliant idea hidden inside a confusing structure will be ignored.

But what is the *right* structure? This is where most writers make critical mistakes. They believe the structure is determined by the topic. For example: "I'm writing an update, so I'll use bullet points". This is writer-centric thinking.

The agile communicator knows that the correct structure is never determined by the topic. It is determined by only one thing: **your target audience's predicted emotional reaction.**

The 3 Structural Patterns

Choosing the right structural pattern or structure is **an act of empathy.** You must first analyze your audience and predict how they will feel after receiving your message and then choose the structure that prepares them for your message most effectively.

Use this "Traffic Light" model to make your decision.

Indirect Structure (Red Light)

- Best for targeting displeased audiences with bad news.
- Cultural Note: Use as the default structure for High Context cultures where "saving face" is critical.
- Logic: Provide the rationale before the bad news to minimize defensiveness and preserve the relationship.

Hybrid Structure (Yellow Light)

- Best for targeting *skeptical* audiences with persuasive or sensitive news.
- Cultural Note: Use as the default structure for internal persuasion and sales.
- Logic: Build a shared context, a *Buffer*, before delivering the main point to reduce resistance to minimum.

Direct Structure (Green Light)

- Best for targeting receptive audiences with positive or non-sensitive news.
- Cultural Note: Use as the default structure in Low Context cultures.
- Logic: Get straight to the point. Speed is respectful.

Before selecting your message structure, remember that many business documents, especially reports and memos, are read by **three types of readers:**

Pro Tip: Write for the Three Types of Readers

Every business document you create will likely be read by three distinct audiences, each with different needs. Your message structure must serve all of them simultaneously:

The Executive (The Skimmer): They are time-poor and decision-focused. They will read the first paragraph, your Executive Summary, or the main point, the bottom line, if it's written clearly and maybe the headings or table of contents. If the bottom line isn't immediately visible, they will stop reading.

- *Strategy:* Put your main point, the bottom line, request, or conclusion in the very first sentence or paragraph. Use clear, bold headings. You may even write: "My Main Point is:" or "The Bottom Line is …" to make it clear what your main point is.

The Assessor (The Skeptic): This is your boss, a peer, or a compliance officer. They need to verify your work. They will read the details to check your logic, data, and methodology.

- *Strategy:* Use a logical structure like Hybrid or Indirect in the body of your message to build your case. Provide evidence, data points, and context to support your claims.

The Researcher (The Miner): This could be a future employee or even you, six months from now. They are looking for specific information or data points buried within the document.

- *Strategy:* Use clear formatting, bullet points, and searchable keywords. Make it easy to scan and retrieve specific details without reading the entire text.

By writing for all three types of readers, you guarantee that your reports and memos will be read and understood by all readers.

Direct Structure for Receptive Audiences

In business, speed is a strategic advantage. By using Direct structure, the writer minimizes the time it takes for the audience to read and understand the message and then act on it.

The Direct structure prioritizes efficiency in communication by immediately presenting the most crucial information first: the main point, the bottom line, conclusion, or request. This structure is the primary tool for achieving efficiency and it is particularly effective for both internal and external communication.

Direct structure should be your default structure for 90% of your messages especially if you live in a Low Context culture.

Bottom Line Up Front (BLUF) Framework.

You deliver the main point first, then provide the supporting details.

- State the Main Point (Bottom Line or Solution): This is the key message, your request, or "ask".
- Provide Context and Supporting Details (Problem or Complication): The necessary background, data, or context.
- End with a Courteous Close (Call to Action): A clear statement of what's up next.

Predicted audience reaction: positive, neutral, or annoyed. It is ideal for positive and non-sensitive messages, as well as for positive persuasive messages that aim to encourage a desired positive outcome. It's also used for internal negative non-persuasive messages for downward communication in low-context cultures.

When to use it: Use it for any "green light" message where the audience is receptive and your news is likely to be well received with minimal or no resistance at all. This includes delivering good news; making routine requests;

answering direct questions; sending routine updates; and writing executive summaries, for example.

Why It Works: It's efficient and respects your reader's time. When the news is good or neutral, the reader wants it immediately. Delaying it with unnecessary background is frustrating.

Case Study: Direct Structure for Positive News

Scenario: Announcing a highly requested employee benefit called: "Flexible Fridays."

- **Target Audience Reaction?** Pleased. This is news they have been asking and waiting for.
- **Desired Outcome?** To inform and celebrate.
- **Required Impact?** Excitement and clarity.
- **Structure: Direct.** Get straight to the good news to maximize the impact.

The Ineffective (Hybrid) Draft

(Message) As you know, our company is always looking for ways to improve work-life balance. We have analyzed the results from the Q3 engagement survey and, after much deliberation by the leadership team, we have been exploring several options...

Why it fails: This is a classic "throat-clearing" opening. The reader is bored and confused by the third sentence. They see a wall of text and have no idea what it's about.

The Effective (Direct) Draft:

- **(Subject)** New Policy: Announcing "Flexible Fridays."
- **(Main Point)** Team, Starting November 1, we are implementing “Flexible Fridays.”
- **(Context & Details)** This has been your #1 request in our last two surveys. Here is how it will work: The core workday will be 8 a.m. to

1 p.m. The afternoon is yours for flexible work, personal appointments, or getting an early start to your weekend, if your client work is complete.

- **(Courteous Close)** Please, review the full policy attached and join a 30-minute Q&A with HR this Thursday.

Hybrid Structure for Skeptical Audiences

The Hybrid structure is a communication model that combines directness with diplomacy. It initiates with a neutral, or positive statement, a buffer, to establish context before presenting the main point.

This approach is crucial when delivering news or making requests that could cause minor inconvenience or disappointment, as not all business situations are straightforward. It is particularly effective in marketing and sales, or when communicating internally and the message is somewhat negative, and the situation needs persuasion to achieve the desired outcome. It also works for negative messages targeting your superiors when no persuasion is needed.

What It Is: This framework builds a logical, somewhat persuasive case before delivering the main point. It's designed to create buy-in by aligning the reader with the problem before you introduce your solution. You open with a buffer, a contract sentence, which doesn't reveal the bottom-line immediately.

- Open with a Buffer (Problem/Complication): Start with a shared problem or opportunity. Use data and examples.
- State the Main Point Clearly (Bottom-Line/Resolution): Introduce your idea as the logical solution to the problem you've just outlined.
- End with a Positive, Forward-Looking Close (Call to Action)

Predicted audience reaction: skeptical, somewhat resistant, or needing to be "warmed up" before stating the main point.

When to Use It: Use this for any "yellow light" message where you need to convince, not just inform. It's perfect for: pitching a project to a skeptical boss; asking for a significant budget increase; trying to get your team to adopt a new (and potentially difficult) process, for example.

Why It Works: It answers the reader's "Why should I?" before they can say "No". A direct request ("I need $150,000") leads to a direct "No" based on cost.

Case Study: Hybrid Structure for Sensitive News

Scenario: Convincing the leadership team to invest $150,000 in new CRM software. They have been hesitant about big tech spending.

- **Audience Reaction?** Skeptical and resistant. They are "allergic" to new tech spending.
- **Goal of the Message?** To get a "yes" for a $150,000 investment.
- **Required Impact?** To make them see this not as a cost, but as a solution to a bigger problem.
- **Selected Structure: Hybrid.** I must align them with the problem (lost time and money) before I ever mention the solution (the new software).

The Ineffective (Direct) Draft

Subject: Request for $150,000 for new CRM **Body:** I am requesting approval to spend $150,000 to purchase the Salesforce CRM...

Why it fails: The reader sees the price tag and immediately thinks "No." Their minds are now closed, and they will spend the rest of the email finding reasons to justify their "No."

The Effective (Hybrid) Draft

- **(Subject)** Solving Our Q4 Sales Lag
- **(Buffer)** Team, I've analyzed our Q4 sales data and found our team is losing an average of 40 hours per week per rep on manual data

entry. (Agitate) This lost productivity equates to $80,000 in sunk costs last quarter and has directly contributed to a 15% lag in our client follow-up times, which is our #1 complaint.

- **(Main Point)** A new CRM platform would automate this entire process. To solve this, I am requesting $150,000 to implement Salesforce, which will reclaim that lost time, cut our follow-up lag to zero, and have a projected ROI of $400,000 in the first year."
- **(Positive, Forward-Looking Close)** "Looking forward to your approval. Yours sincerely, [Your Name]. Indirect Structure for Displeased Audiences

Indirect structure is an empathetic and cautious communication method. It prioritizes building a logical and emotional foundation before presenting a difficult message, effectively inverting the Direct Structure.

This approach is ideal for external communication with customers, business partners, suppliers, and other stakeholders, particularly when delivering negative persuasive or non-persuasive messages.

What It Is: This is the most delicate framework, designed to deliver negative information while minimizing defensiveness and preserving the relationship.

- Open with a Buffer (Situation): Start with a neutral, empathetic, and true statement.
- Provide the Reasoning (Complication or Problem): Explain the reasons for the decision before you deliver the bad news.
- State the Bad News Clearly but Gently (Resolution): Deliver the negative news clearly, concisely, and firmly.
- End with a Helpful, Forward-Looking Close (Call to Action)

Predicted Audience Reaction: Displeased, angry, or disappointed.

When to Use It: Use this for any "red light" message where you must deliver bad news and need to manage a negative emotional reaction. This includes delivering unfavorable decisions to clients, partners, or your superiors; rejecting a proposal or application; and telling a long-time vendor you are not renewing their contract; writing or presenting a report to executives when you need to provide more context and build a persuasive narrative, especially if the audience is unfamiliar with the topic or may be resistant to your solution, for example.

Why It Works: It prepares the reader emotionally. Dropping bad news in the first sentence (Direct Structure) feels like a slap in the face. This structure shows that you are a thoughtful, rational decision-maker. The reader is more likely to accept the logic of the decision, even if they don't like the outcome.

By conveying significant bad news or persuading a resistant audience demands not only clarity but also deep empathy and strategic foresight.

Case Study: Indirect Structure for Bad News

Scenario: Terminating an employment agreement.

1. **Goal of the Message?** To deliver the bad news firmly but empathetically.
2. **Required Impact?** To preserve the relationship and prevent a defensive, angry response.
3. **Selected Structure: Indirect.** I must use a buffer and provide the rationale before the bad news to show respect and demonstrate this was a logical, not personal, decision.

Audience Reaction? Disappointed and possibly angry. This is a long-term partner.

The Ineffective (Direct) Draft

The Direct Structure is used in low context cultures for internal negative non-persuasive messages targeting subordinates if there is no room for negotiation.

Although delivering bad news to your subordinates by using a direct structure may seem counterintuitive, it's a strategic choice for some organizations located typically in low context cultures. These cultures prioritize honesty, efficiency, and clarity, so negative feedback is typically delivered in a blunt, explicit, and straightforward manner, even though it can be perceived as harsh by those from other cultures. Direct negative feedback is valued for its honesty and directness, which is seen as a sign of respect for the truth.

- **(Subject)** Termination Letter
- **(Message)** "Dear [Your Name], Your employment agreement has been terminated due to the inactivation of your business unit. Your last working day is 30 June 2025. Please, contact our HR department to return all company assets. You will receive your last monthly salary and the Certificate of Employment on your last working day. BR, [Boss Name]

Using the Direct Structure may be an "ineffective" way to deliver bad news to your subordinates because it feels "abrupt and disrespectful," which can make the recipient "immediately defensive and angry", and you might risk losing the relationship forever.

A more effective and less risky approach is to use the Indirect Structure, which is designed to deliver negative information while minimizing defensiveness and preserving the relationship.

This Indirect structure follows a clear, four-part model:

1. **Buffer (Situation)** A neutral, empathetic, and true statement.
2. **Rationale (Problem/Complication)** The reasons for the decision, given before the bad news.
3. **Bad News (Solution/Resolution)** The negative news, delivered clearly and firmly.
4. **Close (Call to Action)** A helpful or forward-looking close.

The Effective (Indirect) Draft

- **Subject:** An Update to Your Role
- **(Buffer)** "Hi [Your Name], I'm writing to follow up on our recent discussions about the company's organizational changes. We've genuinely appreciated your contributions as part of the [Team Name] team.
- **(Reasoning)** As you know, the company has been re-evaluating its strategic priorities. After a difficult review, we have made the hard decision to inactivate the team: [Team Name]
- **(Bad News)** Because the role assigned to you is part of that team, your employment agreement will be terminated, effective 30 June 2025.

- **(Helpful, Forward-Looking Close)** We are committed to supporting you through this transition. Our HR department will be in touch shortly to schedule a meeting to discuss severance, support for your job search, and the process for returning company assets. You will receive your final salary and Certificate of Employment on your last working day. Thank you again for your hard work during your time with us. Best, [Manager's Name]

The Persuasive Structures to Guide Your Audience

We've learned that our message's structure must be based on our audience's predicted emotional reaction. We identified three core frameworks:

- The Direct Structure for Receptive Audiences
- The Hybrid Structure for Skeptical Audiences
- The Indirect for Displeased Audiences

All these fundamental audience-centric structures can be used for crafting and conveying persuasive messages; however, persuasion is so critical to business success that it deserves its own deep dive. Now, we're going to explore three famous frameworks:

- The **SCR** framework benefits professionals in multiple industries by promoting clarity, brevity, and impact.
- The **AIDA** Model is the key to writing proposals that get funded, pitches that win clients, and memos that change behavior.
- The **PSB** framework is a simple, three-part argument that states the problem, the solution, and the benefits and makes an immediate and compelling case for a change or action.

The McKinsey SCR Framework

The McKinsey SCR (Situation-Complication-Resolution) framework is a communication structure refined by McKinsey consultants to present ideas logically, persuasively, and efficiently. It mirrors the natural human process of understanding stories or problems: grasping the Situation, identifying Complications, and seeking Resolutions.

This method streamlines complex information, helping audiences quickly understand core issues and proposed paths forward. Its elegant simplicity and consistent results make it popular among consultants, business leaders, and strategic communicators.

There are two variants of the SCR framework: SCQA & SCQR

- **Situation:** Sets the context by describing the current, normal status.
- **Complication:** Introduces the problem that disrupts the status quo.
- **Question:** Poses a question that naturally arises from the complication, which the rest of the communication (the messenger) will answer.
- **Answer/Resolution:** Provides the solution, recommendation, or main conclusion that answers the question.

The McKinsey SCR framework benefits professionals across industries by promoting clarity, brevity, and impact. Unlike disorganized presentations, the framework keeps messaging concise and audience-focused, preventing questions like "Why am I hearing this?" or "What should I do with this information?" It also clarifies one's own thinking, helping to pinpoint which aspects of the situation, problem, and solution to emphasize.

The framework empowers you to tell a curated story and function as an advisor, rather than just delivering raw data to stakeholders. A key aspect of the McKinsey SCR Framework is the audience-specific nature, allowing you to tailor your message to address audience needs and objections.

Furthermore, the frameworks are highly adaptable. It can be used in both spoken and written communication, from summarizing findings in a slide deck to drafting client emails or preparing for sales meetings. This versatility makes it a go-to method for savvy business communicators.

Finally, the McKinsey SCR framework supports rapid thinking and decision-making, which are crucial in today's "Attention Economy" where the primary goal of business communication is to gain buy-in and motivate action.

The SCR Framework in Action

The SCR Framework is a powerful tool used to structure a logical argument or presentation. It first establishes a clear context, then introduces a problem, and finally proposes a solution.

Here is a breakdown of how a team leader might present a problem to senior management using the SCR framework.

Scenario: A Mid-Sized E-commerce Company.

Situation: This is the starting point that answers the audience's first question: "What?" It sets the context and states a fact-based, non-controversial overview of the current state that everyone can agree on. "Dear team, For the past three years, our e-commerce company, 'Swift Buy,' has successfully grown revenue by 20% annually. This growth has been driven by our strong customer loyalty, which is built on our brand name promise of fast, reliable 2-day shipping.

Complication: This answers the audience's second question: "So What?" or "What's in It for Me?" It introduces the challenge, problem, or trigger event that disrupts the stable situation and creates urgency. "However, over the last two quarters, we've seen a sharp decline in our customer satisfaction scores, directly tied to shipping. A new, well-funded competitor has entered our market offering a free 1-day shipping option. Simultaneously, our primary logistics partner just increased their rates by 15%, making our current 2-day shipping model less profitable and slower than the new market standard."

Resolution: This is the proposed, actionable solution that answers the audience's third question: "Now What?" and directly addresses the complication. "To solve this, we must diversify our logistics network. I recommend we immediately form a pilot partnership with two regional, last-mile delivery services to regain our competitive edge in key markets. This will allow us to offer 1-day shipping to 60% of our customers while also reducing our reliance on a single, expensive logistics partner."

The AIDA Model

AIDA is an acronym that has been a cornerstone of marketing and sales for over a century. It stands for Attention, Interest, Desire, and Action. The AIDA model is most widely attributed to Elias St. Elmo Lewis, an American advertising and sales pioneer. He first formulated the concept in 1898. Lewis's original goal was to optimize sales calls by outlining the four cognitive stages a salesperson must lead a prospect through to achieve sales.

AIDA provides step-by-step scaffolding for any persuasive message.

- **Attention:** This is your hook. It's the subject line, the opening sentence, or the headline that stops the reader from scrolling. It must break through the noise by either posing an urgent question, stating a shocking fact, or, most effectively, tapping into a shared problem.
- **Interest:** Once you have their attention, you have a few seconds to earn their interest. This is where you connect the "hook" directly to the reader's world. You build on the problem and show them why it matters to them.
- **Desire:** This is the most critical and emotional step. Interest is logical ("I see this is a problem"). Desire is emotional ("I want this problem to be solved"). You build desire by painting a picture of a better future. You're not selling your solution yet; you're selling the outcome of your solution.
- **Action or Ask:** Only after you have their attention, interest, and desire do you make your request. The Action must be clear, specific, and easy to do.

Never use AIDA for non-persuasive messages.

Using AIDA to "sell" an extra annual bonus is unnecessary or to fire someone is cruel. The goal of the AIDA is to persuade, not to "sell" good or bad news.

AIDA for "Negative Persuasive" Messages

Normally, AIDA is used for selling. But when you need to "sell" a painful change, like a new, mandatory, and complex system, you are facing an uphill battle. This is a "negative persuasive" scenario.

Scenario: You need to get your team to adopt a new, complicated, and mandatory expense reporting system (which they will hate).

The Ineffective (Direct) Approach:

- **(Message)** "Team, from next Monday, we are all required to use the new SAP expense system. All training modules must be completed by Friday."
- **Result:** Everyone complains about how the old system was fine.

The Effective (AIDA-Adapted) Approach:

The Strategy: Use AIDA to bypass the immediate pain and focus entirely on the long-term gain.

- **Attention (The Hook):** Start with a shared pain point to grab their attention: "Team, I know one of our biggest frustrations is how long it takes to get reimbursed for expenses."
- **Interest (The Root Cause):** Explain why the pain exists, validating their frustration: "The root cause is our old system, which requires manual data entry from three different departments. This is why a simple lunch receipt can take 30 days to clear."
- **Desire (The Better Future):** Paint a picture of the solution's outcome—not the tool itself: "What if we could get reimbursed in 48 hours, every time, just by taking a picture of a receipt on our phones? No more spreadsheets, no more waiting."
- **Action (The Ask):** Now that they want the outcome, present the change as the only way to get it: "To make that happen, we are moving to a new SAP system. It is a major change and will require a 2-hour training session from everyone. But it is the only way to solve

our #1 frustration and get everyone paid faster. Here is the link to the training..."

Why It Works: You didn't sell the product (the new system), which they hate. You sold the outcome (getting paid faster), which they desire. AIDA transforms a "have to" into a "want to."

PBS for Marketing & Sales Email Campaigns

While AIDA is powerful for complex persuasion, many situations call for a more direct, logical proposal. For these, the "Problem Solution Benefit" (PBS) framework is a highly effective tool. It is a simple, three-part argument that makes an immediate and compelling case for a change or action. It's logical, persuasive, and respects the reader's time by focusing only on the essential components of your proposal.

- **Problem:** State the issue clearly and concisely, for example, we have lost our funding for the arts program due to budget cuts.
- **Solution:** State your proposed plan to fix the problem, for example, I propose we hold a fundraiser to raise the $50,000 shortfall.
- **Benefit:** Explain the positive outcome that will result., for example, by raising this money, we will be able to produce our final show of the season.

A Strategic Note on Cultural Context

The message structures are not culturally neutral. As we defined in Chapter 2, your choice is a major part of your risk assessment in cultural context.

Direct Structure for Low-Context Cultures

Effective and respectful cultures value speed and explicitness. Low-context cultures are societies that rely on explicit, direct communication where the meaning is in the words themselves, not in the context or non-verbal cues. Key characteristics include valuing individualism, directness, logic, and efficiency, with relationships often being short-term and task oriented.

Low-context cultures typically include Northern European, the Benelux, and German-speaking European countries, as well as the United States, Canada, Israel, Australia, and New Zealand.

Indirect Structure for High-Context Cultures

High-context cultures value saving face, building consensus, and preserving relationships. Using a Direct structure in a high-context business situation is a common strategic error and can be seen as rude or impatient.

High-context cultures are present in France, Southern, Southeastern, and Eastern Europe, as well as Mexico, Central & South America, and Africa. In the Asia-Pacific region, most countries fall into this category, with the exceptions of Israel, Australia, and New Zealand.

Hybrid Structure for Shaping Company Culture

Internal marketing shapes company culture. Sending negative persuasive messages directly can feel harsh, while indirect approaches may seem evasive, so use the Hybrid structure for internal negative persuasive messages and for negative non-persuasive messages targeting your superiors.

In low-context cultures people use Direct structure for crafting and conveying negative *non*-persuasive message targeting subordinates, because it is seen as effective and efficient communication method; however, in high-context cultures a direct approach may feel too harsh, so I recommend using Hybrid structure or the AIDA model instead.

Important Nuance

It's crucial to remember that "high-context" and "low-context" are points on a spectrum, and no culture is exclusively one or the other. There is still variation within each country, and all societies have elements of both.

For example, while most English-speaking countries are considered low-context cultures, the United Kingdom is often seen as having a higher-context communication style compared to countries like the United States, Canada, and Australia that prioritize direct, explicit communication, where messages are clear and unambiguous.

The United Kingdom is often cited as an example of a culture that uses more indirect language, diplomacy, and non-verbal communication than its Anglo-Saxon neighbors. This doesn't mean the UK is a high-context culture, but rather that it falls somewhere between low- and high-context, with a greater reliance on indirectness and non-verbal cues.

The choice is not about what's the easiest message structure for you to write; it's a strategic decision based on empathy.

Your Agile Message Strategy is Set

By answering the questions from Part I, you have completed your **"Step Zero"** You now have a complete, human-led plan.

You know:

- Why do you write (Commander's Intent)
- Who you write for (Audience)
- How you manage authenticity (The Traffic Light)

Answering these questions forces you to be an analyst before you can become a writer. You are now ready to move to execution: choosing your message type based on the right structure, stickiness level, and style. But before we focus on stickiness and style, we'll learn about the Agile Writer's Process: A Role-Based Workflow

CHAPTER 5: THE AGILE WRITER'S PROCESS

In Chapter 2, we established the unbreakable rule: put your reader first. You learned the three foundational questions, Why? Who? and Why will they care, that forms the core of your communication's Desired Outcome.

But having a well-defined desired outcome is only half the battle. The other half is execution. This is where most of us get stuck. We sit down to draft an email or a report, and we try to do everything at once. We brainstorm, outline, draft, edit, and proofread in the same chaotic burst of effort. Our fingers fly, then we hit delete. We write a perfect sentence, then spend ten minutes agonizing over a single word choice.

This "all at once" approach is not just inefficient; it's the root cause of writer's block. It puts the creative, generative part of your brain in direct conflict with the critical, analytical part. But there is a deeper, emotional reason this is so paralyzing: writing is vulnerability. As CEO Kyle Wiens notes, it "exposes the writer's ideas and ability... That makes writing hard and difficult to talk about". We are afraid of "The Editor" before we've even written a word. The result is paralysis.

Why This Writing Process Works

This role-based method is powerful because it uses a "separation of concerns". It prevents your inner Editor from silencing your Researcher before they've had a chance to speak. It turns the overwhelming task of "writing" into a manageable, step-by-step process.

This human-led process is also the key to unlocking the true power of AI. Instead of just asking an AI to "write an email," which gives you a generic and often ineffective result, you can now use it as an assistant in each specific role:

Analyst: " I want to write a business message and deliver it as an email. Function as a professional business communications expert and help me evaluate the cultural context, assess business risks, and analyze my audience against my desired outcome and predict the audience's reaction to my message. The cultural context and business situation is: [Insert a description of the cultural context and business situation here] My audience is [Insert a description of your audience here] and my desired outcome is [Insert the description of the desired outcome or the Commander's Intent Statement here]. Assess the cultural context and business risks and predict the audience's

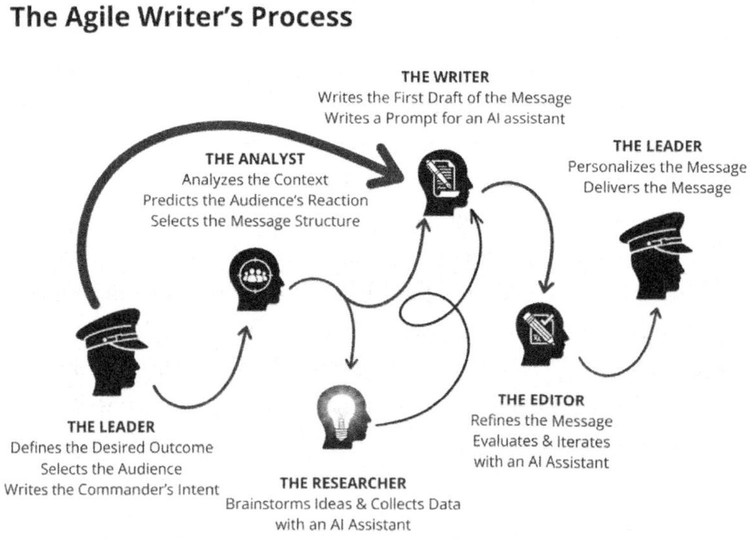

reaction against the desired outcome. Recommend the best message structure, style, and stickiness type for the message and three alternative subject lines for the email."

Researcher: "Function as a professional change consultant. My objective is to introduce a new process to my team and secure their adoption. Please help me by brainstorming two key areas: Potential Resistance: What are all the possible reasons my team might resist this change? and Perceived Benefits: What are all the potential advantages and benefits of this new process for them personally and professionally?"

Writer (Prompter): "Function as a professional business Writer. Draft a complete message based on the recommended message type and the provided raw data. Use the following structure: [Insert the message structure recommended by the Analyst]; type: [Insert the message type recommended by the Analyst], and stickiness: [Insert the stickiness principles recommended by the Analyst]. Here is the raw data: [Insert notes from the Researcher]."

Editor: "Function as an Editor. Review this draft for clarity and conciseness. Identify three sentences that can be made shorter. Please also check the text for any use of jargon and recommend rephrasing."

The Leader is not using AI for defining the desired outcome or personalizing the final message; however, an AI Assistant can be used to evaluate the personalized message created by the Leader and recommend improvements, if needed.

By mastering this process, you stay in the driver's seat. You provide the strategy and manage the workflow, using AI as a powerful assistant to help you be more creative, organized, and polished. In the next chapters, we will dive deeper into the "Analyst" phase, giving you the core structures you need to build any message.

The 5 Professional Roles for Agile Communication

To become an agile and effective communicator, you must stop trying to do all jobs at once and instead separate the writing process into five distinct roles.

Pilot's Workflow Checklist:

1. **The Leader:** Defines the 'Why' and the desired measurable outcome.
2. **The Analyst:** Analyzes the target audience and predicts the 'Red/Yellow/Green' reaction and picks the structure.
3. **The Researcher:** Harvests data and prompts experts (or AI assistants).
4. **The Writer:** Converts the brief into a clear, outcome-driven first draft.
5. **The Editor:** Ruthlessly 'tightens and brightens' the text for maximum impact.
6. **The Leader:** Personalizes the message before sending it.

The Leader Defines the Commander's Intent

The Leader initiates the process. This role is concerned with the high-level key questions: "What?" and "Why?". The Leader selects the target audience, defines the desired outcome, and writes the Commander's Intent Statement.

The Leader Acts as the Editor-in-Chief

The Leader completes the process. This role is concerned with the outcome. The Leader makes sure that the message was crafted according to the Agile Message Strategy and it will convey the Commander's Intent to the target audience. This will minimize the likelihood of producing undesired outcomes.

The Leader writes the Commander's Intent Statement without help from an AI Assistant; however, the Leader can ask the AI Assistant to assess the final statement and then refine it based on the AI recommended improvement ideas before handing it off to the Analyst, Researcher, and Writer.

The Analyst Develops Message Strategy

The Analyst develops the Agile Message Strategy, the principled approach for what to say and how to say it to produce the desired outcome.

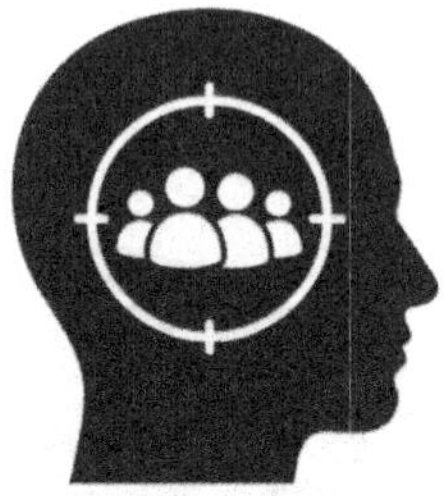

ANALYST

The Analyst conducts deep context analysis of the audience, including trust level, hierarchy, and cultural context. Based on this analysis, the Analyst selects the best message Structure (Direct, Hybrid, Indirect), the required level of Stickiness, and the appropriate Style.

The Analyst also justifies assumptions. This role appreciates what constitutes evidence. When factual data is absent—especially when discussing future developments—the Analyst has the responsibility to explicitly identify and justify the assumptions being made.

The Researcher Gathers Information

The Researcher brainstorms ideas and collects information and data. This is your creative, unfiltered, brainstorming phase. When you wear this hat, there is no judgment. You brainstorm every possible idea, angle, and objection. The goal here is quantity, not quality.

As the Researcher, you can ask your AI Assistant to brainstorm ideas with you and collect all related information, data, and supporting facts. You can give information sources to your AI Assistant to summarize information for you.

RESEARCHER

Beyond using AI to summarize documents, a key modern researcher skill is using AI tools to identify who in the organization holds undocumented, tacit expertise, such as learnings from past failures, and connecting with them, because 80-90% of organizational knowledge is not written down but remains inside people's heads.

Most people use AI only as a search engine. They ask, "How do I improve team culture?" and the AI gives them the average of the internet: generic, bland advice like "have more meetings" or "be respectful." This is the "regression to the mean."

"When you ask AI a generic question, you get a generic answer."

The Agile Researcher knows that to get better answers from your AI Assistant, you must change the source material. You don't want your AI Assistant's opinion; you want it to simulate the world's best thinking.

We call this: "Steering to Experts." This technique forces your AI Assistant to abandon "average" advice and ground its response in specific, high-quality frameworks. There are two ways to prompt: the "Passenger" and the "Pilot":

The Passenger Prompt (Generic Mediocrity): "Explain how to make a team more innovative." Result: A list of clichés about brainstorming and "no bad ideas."

The Pilot Prompt (Steering to Mastery): "Explain how to make a team more innovative using ideas from Pixar's Braintrust, Satya Nadella's growth mindset strategy, and Harvard's research on psychological safety." Result: A specific, actionable framework based on proven methodologies.

Often, you won't know which experts to cite. In that case, use the Researcher role to perform a "Two-Step Synthesis."

Step 1: Expert Identification. Ask your AI Assistant to find the "grand masters" for you. Prompt: "List the top 5 experts, researchers, and foundational books regarding [Topic, e.g., Change Management] from the last 10 years."

Step 2: Expert Synthesis. Once your AI Assistant lists them (e.g., John Kotter, Brene Brown), use them as your filter. Prompt: "Great. Now, using the frameworks from Kotter and Brown, outline a communication plan for my specific change initiative."

By steering your AI Assistant toward mastery, you ensure your message is built on a foundation of credibility, not just internet noise.

The Writer Writes the First Draft

The Writer's job is to draft the message.

The Writer gets the Commander's Intent Statement including the desired outcome from the Leader, the message strategy from the Analyst, and the ideas, information, and data from the Researcher. The Writer translates the strategic decisions from the other roles into a complete first draft.

With this complete strategy brief, the Writer can either write the first draft manually or, more efficiently, function as the "Prompter" and craft an expert-level prompt for an AI Assistant to generate the first draft.

The Writer's Brief

The Writer's Brief includes instructions for the Writer on how to use an AI Writing Assistant:

1. Upload all research notes, data, and background documents to your Notebook.
2. Copy the template below.
3. Replace the [BRACKETED SECTIONS] with the specific details from your Strategy Brief.
4. Paste the completed prompt into the chat box.

The Writer's Prompt Template

The Writer's Prompt Template includes instructions for the Writer on how to write a prompt for an AI Writing Assistant.

The Prompt Template

- **Role:** "Function as a professional business communications assistant."
- **Task:** "The [Insert communicator's name or role] needs a first draft of an outcome-driven message to be sent to:"
- **Target audience:** [Insert a description of your target audience]
- **Business situation:** "Currently, [Describe your current business situation], but the thing is that …"
- **The issue:** [Describe the problem or opportunity]
- **The impact: "**This leads to [Insert implications or consequences due to the opportunity or problem] … "
- **The value:** "saving/costing [Insert the target] time/money about [Insert the amount/value] …"
- **The desired outcome:** "Therefore, the objective is to [Insert the desired measurable outcome] … "
- **The solution:** "by [Insert the solution],"
- **The purpose:** "because it's important to [Insert the purpose]"
- **The sources:** "Use all uploaded sources and the information provided above to generate a clear, concise, and professional-looking first draft that drives the audience towards the desired outcome."

A Prompt Example

"Function as a professional business communications assistant. The [CEO of ABC Co., Ltd.] needs a first draft of an outcome-driven message to be sent to [his direct reports]. Currently, [CEOs are spending 61% of work time effectively on face-to-face interactions; however, the remaining 39% is spent inefficiently on non-face-to-face interactions: talking the phone, reading and replying to written correspondence, and managing electronic communications], but the thing is that [unclear messaging is the reason for miscommunication and it's ruining our productivity]. This leads to [wasting time on non-face-to-face interactions], costing [the CEO and his direct reports] about [1,200 hours a year]. Therefore, the objective is to [learn to write clear, concise, and professional-looking business messages efficiently with the help of AI], by [coaching all employees the fundamentals of strategic messaging and how to use AI Assistants to help write and edit messages], because it's important to [stop wasting time on inefficient non-face-to-face interactions and reclaim the time for effective face-to-face interactions with people we work with, our family members and friends]. Use all uploaded sources and information provided to generate a clear, concise, and professional-looking first draft that drives the audience towards the desired outcome."

The First Draft

Here is the first draft the AI Assistant wrote based on the Writer's prompt:

Subject: Reclaiming 1,200 Hours: Our New Standard for Communication

(Situation) Team, time is our most finite resource. As senior leaders, we invest 61% of our working hours in high-value, face-to-face interactions with our customers, partners, and suppliers. This is time well spent. However, the remaining 39% of our time, devoted to non-face-to-face interactions like email, reports, and memos, is facing a critical efficiency crisis.

(Complication/Problem) The Hidden Cost of "Bad Writing" Ineffective communication is the villain in our productivity story. Messages that are unclear, lack a specific call to action, or require multiple readings to decipher are not just annoying; they are expensive. Current data indicates that poor writing is costing this leadership team **over 1,200 hours a year.** That is 1,200 hours spent deciphering intent rather than driving strategy.

(Resolution/Solution) AI-Augmented Clarity We are drawing a line under this waste. Our objective is to master the art of effective, efficient business messaging. To achieve this, we are launching an initiative with two core pillars:

Back to Fundamentals: We will roll out training for all employees on the core principles of business writing—brevity, clarity, and outcome-orientation.

AI Integration: We will deploy AI Assistants to aid in drafting, editing, and summarizing communications. These tools will ensure every message sent is concise and actionable before it hits an inbox.

(The Why/Authority) This initiative is not about squeezing more work into the day. It is about stopping the waste of time.

(Personalize/Empathy) I want those 1,200 hours back. I want us to stop wasting time on inefficient screens so we can use that saved time for what truly matters: interacting with our families and friends.

(Call to Action) I ask for your full commitment to adopting these tools and setting this new standard within your respective divisions.

(Close) Let's make every word count. Best regards, [CEO Name]

The Editor Refines the Message

The Editor refines the draft by evaluating and iterating the message. The Editor is your critical, analytical filter. The Editor's job is to polish, refine, and cut. This is the only time you are allowed to be negative. They check for clarity, concision, grammar, and tone. They ask the hard questions: "Is this persuasive?" "Is this clear?" "Does this directly serve the Leader's Desired Outcome?". The Editor can ask help from the AI Assistant, if needed.

The Editor can also repurpose the message by changing the target audience, for example. Let's refine the message targeting employees. Here is the Editor's prompt:

"Write another version of this message targeting the employees of the company. Currently, the employees are working overtime and are probably somewhat skeptical of this new initiative, so they are asking what's in it for me?

The Editor's Checklist for AI

The Editor transforms the AI Assistant's "First Draft" into a "Final Message." By evaluating and iterating the message as many times as needed.

Editor's mindset is: "Trust AI Assistant but always verify sources." AI Assistants are fast "thinkers" and writers, but they are not smart. You function as the Editor and control the quality.

Phase 1: Accuracy & Logic (The "BS" Check): Before you fix the words, fix the facts.

- **The Hallucination Scan:** Did the AI Assistant invent any names, dates, or data points? Manually verify every number and URL. If it cites a source, click the link.
- **The Logic Test:** Does the argument make sense? Read the first and last sentence of every paragraph. Do they connect logically? AI often "drifts" and loses the main point.
- **The "Generic Advice" Filter:** Did the AI give specific, actionable advice, or just platitudes? If it said, *"improve communication,"* change it to *"send a weekly email."* Make every vague noun a concrete action.

Phase 2: Tone & Style (The "Robot" Check): Make it sound like a human, not a corporate press release.

- **I Hope This Finds You Well Purge:** Delete all generic, robotic openers. Start directly with the topic or a genuine human greeting.
- **The Adverb Slash:** AI loves words like "crucially," "importantly," and "additionally." Delete 90% of them. They clutter the message.
- **The Passive Voice Hunt:** Search for "was," "were," and "by." Change *"The decision was made by the team"* to *"The team decided."* Active voice owns the action.

- **The Happy Talk Review:** Is the tone too relentlessly cheerful? If the news is neutral or bad, strip away the "excitement" exclamation points. Match the tone to reality.

Phase 3: Strategy Alignment (The Why & What Check): Does this achieve the Commander's Intent?

- **The One-Idea Rule:** Does the message have one clear main point? If there are three main points, cut two or split them into separate messages.
- **The Call to Action (CTA):** Is the next step impossible to misunderstand? Ensure the CTA is specific: *"Reply by Friday"* rather than vague *"Let me know your thoughts"*.
- **So What? Test:** If a busy executive reads only the first paragraph, would they know why this matters? If not, then move the "So What?", the risk or opportunity, to the top of the message.

Phase 4: The Tighten & Brighten Toolkit Apply these specific edits to make the message precise and agile.

- **Kill the Of Monster:** Search for "of the" and "in the" Change *"The purpose of the meeting"* to *"The meeting's purpose,"* change *"The manager of the project"* to *"The Project Manager."* Why should you do this? Because it removes drag, increases reading speed, and makes the message more agile.
- **Exorcise the Zombie Nouns (Nominalizations):** Search for words ending in "-tion," "-ment," and "-ance. Change *"We made a determination"* to *"We determined,"* change *"The implementation of the plan"* to *"Implementing the plan."* Why should you do this? Because it turns static nouns back into active verbs and makes the message precise.
- **The Be-Verb Ban:** Search for "is," "are," "was," and "were." Change *"This is impactful for our sales"* to *"This impacts our sales."* Why should you do this? Because it forces you to use stronger, more descriptive verbs, and makes the messages bright.
- **The Final Read Aloud Test** Read the message aloud. If you stumble, or if it sounds like something a chatbot would say, rewrite that sentence. Your ears are smarter than your eyes.

The Refined Message

The Editor and the AI-Assistant refined the message together:

(Subject) Why we are working late (and how to stop)

(Situation/Attention) Team, I know many of you are working long hours. I see the timestamps on emails sent late at night and over weekends. While I appreciate your dedication, I also know that sustainable high performance requires rest.

(Complication/Interest/Problem) We have analyzed why we spend so much time at our desks. A massive contributor isn't the core work itself; it's the time spent wrestling with unclear communication.

(Desire/Agitate Problem) The Real Villain is the "Back-and-Forth." How often do you stay late because instructions are vague? How much time do you lose trying to decipher a confusing email chain or rewriting a report that missed the mark? Ineffective writing is a hidden tax on your time. It forces you to work longer just to clarify what needs to be done.

(Resolution/Action/Solution) Our Solution is AI-Augmented Communication. To combat this, we are launching a company-wide initiative to upgrade how we read and write messages and use new AI writing assistants.

(Question) You might be asking: "Is this just another tool I must learn?"

(Answer) Here is the reality: AI Assistants will do heavy lifting: They will help you draft clear, concise, professional-looking emails in seconds and summarize long email threads instantly. Training will set clear standards: We are getting back to basics, so you receive clear instructions the first time, reducing the need for endless clarification meetings.

(Benefits) You might be asking: *"What's in it for me?"* The goal of this initiative is not to cram more work into your day. The goal is to eliminate the hours wasted due to miscommunication so you can get your work done effectively and efficiently and leave for home on time.

(Call to Action) I want us to stop working overtime and minimize the time it takes to read and write messages so we can use the saved time for what matters most: being with our families, our friends, and recharging our lives outside of work.

(Close) Thank you for your hard work, now let's get your time back. Best regards, [CEO Name]

The refined message embeds several frameworks simultaneously.

- SCR (Situation, Complication, Resolution)
- AIDA (Attention, Interest, Desire, Action)
- SCQA (Situation, Complication, Question, Answer)
- PSB (Problem, Solution, Benefits)

Agile Communicators, the Writers and the Editors, know how to maximize the impact of messages when needed.

The Leader Personalizes the Message

The Leader concludes the writing process. At the very end of the process, the Leader returns to perform the final, non-negotiable personalization step, adding the authentic voice and empathy needed to build trust. The Leader personalizes the message with the final human touch by adding specific details only the Leader knows.

The Personalization Cheat Code: The Leader can ask the AI Assistant to assess the final personalized message and then refine it once more based on the AI recommended improvement ideas before delivering the final message to the target audience.

Now the Leader can only hope that the message produces the desired outcome and meets the success criteria.

LEADER

CHAPTER 6: THE AGILE DECISION-MAKING PROCESS

In the last four chapters, we've built a powerful toolkit for proactive, human-led communication. But as we established in the introduction, markets shift, crises hit, and audiences react in unpredictable ways. This is the "agile imperative."

Agile Communicator's Core Values

To be an agile communicator, we must be able to adapt and react quickly. The original principles for being agile were defined in 2001, not for communicators, but for software developers. Here are four adapted core values for the Agile Communicator:

- Message Outcomes over Comprehensive Prose
- Audience Collaboration over One-Way Broadcasting
- Human Strategy over Automated Tools (AI)
- Responding to Feedback over Following a Script

Message Outcomes over Comprehensive Prose A 10-page, jargon-filled report ("comprehensive documentation") that no one reads is a failure. A two-sentence email that gets the exact desired outcome ("working software") is a success. This is the essence of our "Craft of Refining" (Chapter 9) and our focus on the "Desired Outcome" (Chapter 2).

Audience Collaboration over One-Way Broadcasting "Broadcasting" is a writer-centric, "fire and forget" message. "Collaboration" is a reader-centric loop. It requires the deep "Audience Analysis" (Chapter 2) and empathy we've discussed, and it treats the audience's feedback as the most critical part of the process.

Human Strategy over Automated Tools (AI) This is the core thesis of this book. A tool, whether it's an email template or a powerful AI, is just an accelerator. Strategy, empathy, and authenticity must come from the human (the "Leader" and "Analyst"). This value is the "why" behind our "Strategy -> Prompt -> Refine -> Personalize" workflow (Chapter 17).

Responding to Feedback over Following a Script This is the skill that separates agile leaders from rigid managers. You cannot just "follow a plan" when a crisis hits or your message is misunderstood. You must be able to observe the new reality, re-orient your strategy, and act. To do this, you need a decision-making model built for speed and adaptation. That framework is the OODA Loop.

OODA Loop

The OODA Loop is a decision-making model developed by a military strategist and U.S. Air Force Colonel John Boyd. Colonel Boyd was a legendary fighter pilot known as "40-Second Boyd" because he could win any dogfight in under 40 seconds. He did this not by being a better pilot, but by being a faster thinker. He developed a model called the OODA Loop to explain how humans make decisions in high-stakes, fluid environments. It stands for:

- **O**bserve,
- **O**rient,
- **D**ecide, and
- **A**ct.

OBSERVE: You gather information and collect raw data from your environment. What's happening? What are the facts?

ORIENT: This is the most important step, the "Strategy First" step. This is where you interpret and filter the gathered information and the collected raw data. You apply your knowledge, experience, and skills to analyze the cultural context, the audience, and the business situation. Use strategic filters to make sense of what you're observing. This is not just seeing, it's understanding.

DECIDE: Based on your orientation, you determine a course of action. You make a choice based on the frameworks from Chapter 2 or 3.

ACT: You execute the decision. This is where you "ship" the email, post the update, or make the call.

Then immediately, the loop begins again.

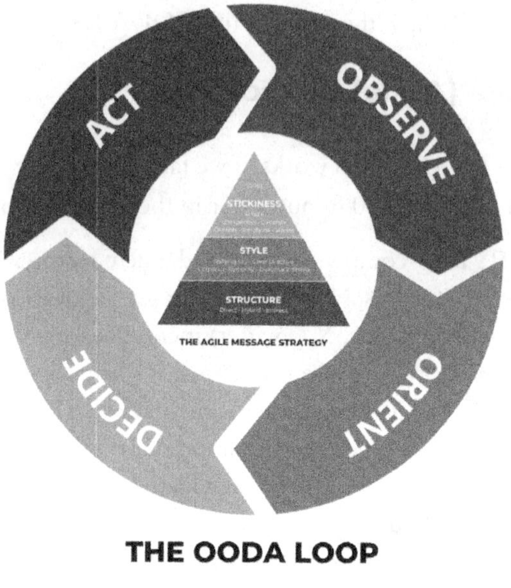

THE OODA LOOP

How to Apply OODA Loop to Crisis Communication

The Scenario: You are a department head.

- A key competitor just launched a new feature that matches your product's main selling point, and they are offering it for 30% less.
- Your sales team is forwarding you panicked emails from clients. Social media is starting to light up.

The Ineffective (Reactive) Response: You immediately fired off an angry email to your engineering team and a defensive, data-dump email to your sales team:

- *"Why didn't we see this coming?!"*
- *"Tell clients, our feature is better!"*

You skipped the Orient and Decide steps. You just Observed and Acted. You created chaos. Think twice before you react. Ask yourself: *"Should I react or reply to this message?"* If your answer is: *"No."*, then don't. If your answer is *"Yes, I should."*, then follow the steps of the OODA Loop.

The Effective (Agile) Response:

Let's see how the OODA Loop works, if we take all four steps, before we write the messages. It takes only 10 minutes to run the OODA loop.

- **OBSERVE:** A competitor launched a new feature. Their price is $29/month. Ours is $49/month. Our top 3 salespeople have emailed in the last 15 minutes. X (Twitter) mentions are up 200%. The competitor's press release is on 3 major tech blogs.
- **ORIENT:** I've looked at their launch video. This is not just a new feature launch; it's a direct assault on our market position. Their feature is new, but it's missing key features: integration with Salesforce and our 24/7 support. This isn't a price war. It's a value war. **My sales team is my priority.** They are scared and need

talking points. **Our clients are my second priority.** They are confused and skeptical. They need reassurance and persuasion.
- **DECIDE:** Strategic thinking and decisions. **Internal Needs:** I will send an email to the sales team. The goal is reassurance and action. I will use the Direct Structure (Chapter 3) to give them clear talking points. **External Needs:** I will write a blog post for our customers. The goal is persuasion. I will use the AIDA Model (Chapter 4) to reinforce our unique value (support and integration) and make them desire our superior solution, not the cheap alternative.
- **ACT:** Task management based on decisions. I'll send the internal memo by email in 10 minutes and publish the blog post in 25 minutes.

Now, you can't control the reactions of your sales team nor your customers, when they receive and read your message, so you just have to wait for the reactions to your email and blog post, observe the reactions or replies, orient to the new sentiment, and the loop continues, but *you* are in control of *your* messages.

How AI Accelerates the OODA Loop

The OODA Loop is a powerful human framework, but it's limited by the speed at which you, a single person, can observe and orient.

This is where AI becomes your *strategic* Assistant, supercharging your loop. In a crisis, you don't have time to manually read 200 tweets or sift through 50 panicked emails. AI can do this for you.

AI-Accelerated Observation

AI can synthesize vast amounts of data in seconds.

- Example Prompt: "Summarize the social media sentiment regarding our company and Competitor X over the last hour. Identify the top 5 questions customers are asking."

AI-Accelerated Orientation & Decision

This is still your job; you set the message strategy. But your AI Assistant can accelerate your analysis and help you generate options fast.

- Example Prompt: "Function as a strategist. Review these 3 competitor emails. Orient me: What is their core strategy, and what is the single biggest weakness we can exploit?"

AI-Accelerated Action

Once you've decided on a message structure, for example, Direct Structure for internal and AIDA for external messages, AI can execute the first draft acting as the "Writer" (Chapter 5) at lightning speed.

- Example Prompt: "Draft an email to my sales team using the Direct Structure. Use forceful, personal, and colorful style. The main point is that we are competing on value, not price. Give them 3 clear talking points."

With AI as your Assistant, your OODA Loop doesn't take 10 minutes. It takes 90 seconds. You can Observe, Orient, Decide, and Act before your competitor even understands the reaction to their own launch.

This is the power of the agile communicator.

CHAPTER 7: THE CONCLUSION TO PART I

You are now equipped with the Analyst's toolkit.

You should remember the unbreakable rule of putting your reader first (Chapter 2), you have a set of powerful, audience-centric structures (Chapters 3-4) for any situation, and you have a process for managing your work (Chapter 5) and for making decisions in high-stakes, fluid environments (Chapter 6).

Answer these questions before you move on to Part II:

- **Do you have your Commander's Intent?** Do you know why you are writing and what your desired outcome is?
- **Do you know your Audience?** Do you know who they are and what they care about?
- **Have you chosen your Traffic Light Structure?** Do you know how you will organize the message based on their predicted reaction?

If you can answer these questions, you know how to select the right message structure that most likely produces your desired outcome.

But a structure alone is not a complete message strategy. In the next section, we focus on the "how": the six stickiness principles and four styles for your messages.

Messaging Made Agile

Strategy First, AI Second

Part II: Crafting the Message

Jorma Manninen

BUSINESS MADE AGILE

WWW.BUSINESSMADEAGILE.COM

PART II EXECUTIVE SUMMARY: THE WRITER'S TOOLKIT

THE BOTTOM LINE

Logic alone is dead on arrival. While Part I built the strategic skeleton, Part II provides the flesh (Stickiness) and skin (Style). Precision communication requires more than just being understood, it requires being remembered and accepted. "Craft" is where human leaders retain their competitive advantage.

KEY TAKEAWAYS

The Neurobiology of Stickiness (SUCCES Model) A message only works if it activates the reader's reward circuit. Use the six principles to move beyond broadcasting data:

- **Simple & Concrete:** To help them understand.
- **Unexpected:** To grab their attention.
- **Credible & Emotional:** To make them believe and care.
- **Stories:** The "flight simulator" that bundles all principles into action.

The StoryBrand (SB7) Pivot Stop being the Hero! Position your *audience* as the **Hero** and yourself as the **Guide.** Provide a simple 3 to 4 step plan that helps them get out of the problematic situation, avoid failure, and achieve success.

The Style Toolkit Style is a strategic choice, not a default voice. Calibrate your message across three spectrums (Authority, Relationship, Engagement) to create:

- The Rallying Cry: To inspire.
- The Clear Directive: To manage.
- The Corporate Authority: To mandate.
- The Diplomatic Shield: To protect.

The Craft of Refining (Tighten & Brighten) Brevity is a sign of respect. High "processing fluency" makes you appear more credible.

Be ruthless and eliminate:

- **Zombie Nouns:** Turn "-tion" and "-ment" words back into active verbs.
- **The "Of" Monster:** Cut prepositional clutter to increase reading momentum.
- **Jargon:** Swap "synergize" and "leverage" for Plain English.

THE CRAFT READINESS CHECKLIST

- Does my message have an "Unexpected" hook?
- Is the reader the Hero of this story? (Am I the Guide?)
- Have I selected the correct Style for the audience's state of mind?
- Have I performed the "Read It Out Loud"(RIOL) test?

PRO-TIP: THE READ IT OUT LOUD TEST

Before you hit send on any high-stakes message, **Read It Out Loud (RIOL).** Your ears are smarter than your eyes. If you stumble over a sentence, lose your breath, or find yourself sounding like a corporate robot, your reader will too.

If it doesn't sound like a human conversation, **rewrite it.**

CHAPTER 8: INTRODUCTION TO PART II

In Part I, you mastered the science of strategy. You learned how to think like an Analyst, define your Commander's Intent, and choose the perfect structure for your message. You now have a solid blueprint. But a blueprint is not a building.

From Blueprint to Building.

A message can have a perfect logical structure and still be dead on arrival. It can be clear but boring. It can be understood today but forgotten by tomorrow.

To make your message live—to make it travel through your organization and change behavior—you need more than logic. You need craft.

Structure is Logic. Style is Emotion.

Part II is your "Writer's Toolkit." It is designed to take your strategic skeleton and give it flesh (Stickiness) and skin (Style).

In the age of AI, this is where you win. An AI can generate a logical structure in seconds. But only a human leader can inject specific, sticky, stylistic choices that make a message resonate.

Your Mission

In this section, you will move from planning the message to building it. You will master three specific crafts that separate the average manager from the visionary leader:

You will master the Science of Stickiness (Chapter 9) You will learn why some ideas survive while others die. You will master the SUCCES Model to make your messages unforgettable and the StoryBrand Framework to make your reader the hero of the journey. You will stop broadcasting data and start broadcasting meaning.

You will master the Psychology of Influence (Chapter 10) You will learn to pull the "invisible levers" of persuasion: Reciprocity, Commitment, Social Proof, Liking, Authority, and Scarcity. You will move beyond logical agreement and discover how to apply scientific principles to move your audience from passive reading to active commitment.

You will master the Art of Style (Chapter 11) You will stop guessing at your "tone of voice." You will learn to strategically select the right Style Combination—from the inspiring "Rallying Cry" to the careful "Diplomatic Shield"—to match the exact emotional needs of your audience.

You will master the Craft of Refining (Chapter 12) You will learn the discipline of brevity. You will discover how to "tighten and brighten" your writing, ruthlessly eliminating the corporate jargon and "slop" that kills trust. You will learn that brevity is not just about saving space; it is a sign of respect for your reader.

You have the strategy. Now let's build the message.

CHAPTER 9: THE CRAFT OF "STICKINESS"

In the first part of this book, "We've built the strategic 'bones' of your message. But a skeleton can't walk on its own. A message can have perfect structure and still be dead on arrival, clear but boring, understood today but forgotten by tomorrow. To make it live, we need to **make an impact.**

Don't just be heard.
Make it stick.

Then why do some messages stick while others fade away? The answer isn't magic; it's neurobiology.

Good Writing is Applied Science

When you read a dull, abstract, jargon-filled memo, your brain's language-processing centers light up. They decode the words, find the meaning, and move on. It's a technical, logical task.

But when you read something truly compelling, a message that is vivid, surprising, and human, something entirely different happens. The message doesn't just get processed; it gets experienced.

What is the effect of reading a well-written message? You get a hit of dopamine, the neurotransmitter for motivation, focus, and pleasure.

The SUCCES Model

Good writing isn't just a communication tool; it's a way to activate your reader's brain's reward circuit. A "sticky" message, therefore, is one that stops being ink on a page and becomes an event inside your reader's mind.

How do we create this neurochemical reaction? We can use a practical, proven toolkit. Authors Chip and Dan Heath, in their groundbreaking book “Made to Stick”, reverse-engineered thousands of "sticky" ideas. The result is one of the most powerful communication frameworks ever created: the SUCCES model.

This framework is so effective because it directly addresses the five sequential actions your target audience must take for a message to become truly sticky and lead to a result:

1. Pay Attention: If you don't get their attention, your message is dead on arrival.
2. Understand & Remember: If they don't grasp your idea, they can't act on it.
3. Believe: If they don't find your message credible, they will dismiss it.
4. Care: If they don't feel an emotional connection, they will be not motivated to act.
5. Act: If they don't know what to do next, the message has no purpose.

The SUCCES model is the practical "how-to" for achieving each of these five outcomes. The principles map directly:

- To make them Pay Attention, be Unexpected.
- To make them Understand & Remember, keep it Simple & Concrete.
- To make them Believe, be Credible.
- To make them Care, be Emotional.
- To help them Act, tell Stories.

We will use this as our practical checklist for making any message memorable, using the science of the brain as our guide.

The 6 Stickiness Principles

A "sticky" idea is one that survives the noise of the inbox and stays with the reader. To achieve this, an idea must incorporate most, if not all, of the following six principles.

Simple: Simplicity is not about "dumbing down" your message; it is about prioritization. It is the ruthless act of stripping an idea down to its critical essence, much like a "Commander's Intent Statement" in the military context. You must discard the peripheral to reveal the core. The human brain craves clarity and elegance. Simple, focused messages are easier to process, which the brain intuitively interprets as being truer and more trustworthy.

Unexpected: To capture attention, you must break a pattern. If your message sounds like everything else, it will be ignored. Great public speakers begin with a surprise. You must use an unexpected "hook" to violate the reader's expectations and create a compelling "knowledge gap", an open loop that they feel driven to close. The brain is fundamentally a prediction machine. When you break its predictions, you trigger a biological attention surge. This releases dopamine, the chemical signal for learning, which tells the brain: "This is important, pay attention and remember it!"

Concrete: Abstract language and words like "synergy", or "world-class service" slides off the brain. Concrete language like "we replace lost items before you hang up the phone" sticks. To make ideas memorable, you must appeal to specific senses. Specific sensory information—like "the squeal of tires" or "the smell of popcorn", activates the reader's sensory and motor cortex. This neural activation allows the reader to physically "feel" the idea, anchoring it deeply in memory.

Credible: For an audience to act, they must believe. Credibility can come from external authority like experts or "anti-authority" like human experiences. However, the most powerful credibility comes from "smart thinking," offering a fresh perspective or a new insight that makes the reader say, "A-ha!" The brain loves to learn. When your message teaches the reader something new and verifiable, it delivers a neurochemical reward. This intellectual satisfaction naturally builds trust in the messenger.

Emotional: We are wired to feel for people, not for data. You cannot inspire engagement with abstract numbers alone. To motivate action, you must tap into fundamental human emotions by focusing on the "who," not just the "what." Humans are social animals. Messages that leverage our social nature—using characters, dialogue, and vivid metaphors—trigger our natural empathy. This emotional resonance is often the deciding factor in moving from agreement to action.

Stories: Storytelling is the primary principle. It is the ultimate delivery vehicle that bundles the other five principles: Simple, Unexpected, Concrete, Credible, and Emotional, into a single, cohesive package that is easy to absorb and retell. The story is a "flight simulator for the brain." It allows the reader to simulate the experience without risk. It is the brain's native operating system for data transfer, making it the most effective way to help people make sense of the world.

A Practical Technique: Using "Callbacks"

Research shows that people forget much of what they experience within a day. To combat this, you can use a "callback", a strategically chosen sentence or phrase that refers to an earlier point. This tactic activates brain circuits involved in forming new memories, helping readers retain more information and "chunk" new content with what they've already learned. For example, if your unexpected hook is: "This isn't a price war; it's a value war", you can call back to it in your conclusion: "This is why we'll win the value war."

Deep Dive: How to Tell Stories?

Most business communication fails because it makes you, your product, or your company a Hero of the story. Harsh truth of life is that your audience doesn't care about you. They care about themselves. They are Heros of their own story, and they are looking for a Guide to help them solve their problem.

Your audience is the Hero.
Position yourself as the Guide.

The 7 Steps of the StoryBrand (SB7) Framework

The StoryBrand SB7 Framework is a 7-step process for building a narrative that makes your audience, the Hero and casts you, or your product, service, or idea as the Guide. The core premise of StoryBrand is a revolutionary flip of the script that directly reinforces the "Unbreakable Rule" from Chapter 2:

Step 1: A Character is the Hero

This is your customer, your boss, or your direct report, or another stakeholder, for example. First, you must find out what the audience wants to hear so that you can predict how they will react to your message.

- Bad Example: "Our customers want to learn to write better messages."
- Good Example: "Our customers want to minimize the time it takes to write messages that most likely produce the desired outcome."

Next, you must find out what their problems are."

The StoryBrand 7-Part Framework

Step 2: The Hero has a Problem

You must identify your audience's problem. The story begins when the Hero has a problem or like Donald Miller, the creator of the StoryBrand framework, often says: "The Hero falls in hole."

Agile Communicators know these problems exist on three levels:

External Problem (The Tangible Issue) This is the physical, practical, or financial result of the problem. It is the "thing" that goes wrong in the real world.

- Example: A poorly written safety memo is misunderstood by factory workers, leading to a machinery malfunction that halts production for three days and costs the company $50,000 in repairs.

Internal Problem (The Emotional Cost) This is how the problem makes the reader (or the writer) of the message feel. It addresses the psychological impact of confusion or rejection.

- Example: Because the manager's feedback on a report was vague and harsh, "rewrite this, it's a bad report", the employee feels anxious, incompetent, and resentful, because the manager couldn't tell how to rewrite the report and what is "a bad report", leading to a loss of morale and a fear of submitting future work.

Philosophical Problem (The deeper "Why it matters") This addresses the moral injustice or the "bigger picture" failure. It answers the question: "Why is it wrong that this problem exists?"

- Example: It is philosophically wrong for a good idea to fail simply because it was communicated poorly

Step 3: The Hero Meets a Guide

Position yourself as the Guide. The Hero is stuck.

Agile Communicators know how to show empathy & authority in this situation.

The Scenario: An intelligent team member feels undervalued because their reports are often ignored or criticized for being confusing or "bad."

- **Show Empathy:** "I know how discouraging it is to spend weeks on a project, only to have the leadership gloss over your recommendations. It feels like your expertise is being ignored, which is incredibly frustrating."
- **Demonstrate Authority:** "However, the issue isn't your analysis; it's the delivery. Your data is solid, but it's buried. We are going to restructure your next report using the 'Bottom Line Up Front' method and we'll add an executive summary for leaders, who just want to know the results and don't have to read the whole report. Once we clear away the clutter, your insights will be impossible to ignore."

Step 4: The Guide Gives a Plan to the Hero

Your idea, product or service is the Plan. The Guide has knowledge, skills, and experience and knows how to solve the Hero's problem, but the Guide mustn't solve the problem on behalf of the Hero. The Guide must clear the fog of confusion and give the Hero a simple 3- or 4-step plan.

Step 5: The Guide Calls to Action

You must ask the Hero to take the first step. The Guide's Call to Action (CTA) must be clear and direct.

Here are examples of the CEO's calls to action:

- **The "Sent Items" Audit:** Spend 15 minutes reviewing your last 10 emails. If the "bottom line" isn't in the first two sentences, rewrite one as a "Model Email" and forward it to your Chief of Staff or direct reports with the note: "This is the standard for clarity I want us to aim for."
- **The "Red Pen" Session:** In your next executive team meeting, project a dense, jargon-filled internal report without author's name on it on the screen. Live edit it together for 10 minutes to make it clear using plain English words. This sets a visual standard for what you expect.
- **The "Sparring Partner" Protocol:** Mandate that for the next week, every strategic memo submitted to you must include a "Devil's Advocate" section generated by AI. This proves the team has considered counterarguments and isn't just selling you on an idea.

Step 6: The Plan Helps the Hero Avoid Failure

You must tell what will happen if the Hero doesn't follow your plan. These are the "stakes:" It's "The Cost of Doing Nothing". If the Hero chooses to ignore the problem, the costs are real:

Here are examples of the CEO's Stakes:

- **Operational Drag (The "Speed Tax"):** Every confusing email triggers a "clarification meeting." If your 100-person team wastes just 2 hours a week deciphering bad instructions, you are burning over 10,000 hours of productivity a year.
- **The "Smartest Person" Paradox:** Your best talent will stop pitching ideas. When high performers feel their innovative proposals are constantly rejected because they can't "break through the noise," they don't get better at writing, they get quiet, or in worst case they quit.
- **Strategic Drift:** Your vision will be misinterpreted. If your "Commander's Intent" is vague, your team will execute what they think you said, not what you meant. This alignment gap grows wider with every layer of management, leading to execution that is completely off target.

Step 7: The Hero Ends in Success

Define what success looks like. Paint a vivid, concrete picture of what the Hero's life looks like after their problem is solved.

Here are examples of the CEO's Wins: The ROI of Clear Communication:

- **The "One-Touch" Decision:** You'll save a lot of time, because speed increases dramatically. You read a memo once, understand the trade-offs immediately, and approve it in 2 minutes. No "let's discuss" meetings required.
- **Innovation Unlock:** The best ideas rise to the top, regardless of who owns them. When writing is standardized, you judge the logic, not the charisma. Quiet introverts with brilliant strategies suddenly have a voice equal to the loudest extroverts.
- **High-Fidelity Execution:** Your strategy scales without distortion. Whether you have 50 employees or 5,000, the "Commander's Intent" travels from the boardroom to the front line with 100% signal strength. The entry-level rep knows exactly why they are doing what they are doing. And managers know how to coach their teams to craft and convey business messages that produce desired outcomes.

Strategic Application: The Stickiness Scale

Now you know how to define your desired outcome, analyze your target audience, select the right structure, and make your message stick. But not all messages are created equal, and not all messages need to stick. By applying all these principles to email scheduling, a meeting is a waste of time and will confuse your reader.

Your job as an agile communicator is to first decide how much stickiness your message needs, and then to select the right tools to get the job done properly.

Very Low Stickiness (2-4 out of 10):

- **Goal:** For messages of finality and closure. The goal is unambiguous clarity, not memorability, allowing the recipient to move on.
- **Message Types:** Internal & External negative non-persuasive messages targeting your superiors (upward) or customers, suppliers, or other (external) stakeholders.
- **Use Cases:** Rejection letters, final warnings, delivering legally sensitive negative news.
- **Key Principles:** Simple and Credible.

Average Stickiness (5-6 out of 10):

- **Goal:** For standard professional messages that must be complied with and considered carefully. The goal is to be understood and taken seriously.
- **Message Types:** Internal negative persuasive messages targeting your superiors (upward) or subordinates (downward) and negative non-persuasive messages targeting your subordinates (downward) as well as external negative persuasive messages targeting your customers, suppliers, or other (external) stakeholders.

- **Use Cases:** Announcing a new (but somewhat inconvenient) process, pitching a project to a skeptical boss, delivering negative feedback, for example.
- **Key Principles:** Simple, Credible, and Concrete.

Very High Stickiness (8-10 out of 10):

- **Goal:** For your most important, high-stakes communication designed to inspire, persuade, and drive enthusiastic action.
- **Message types:** Positive non-persuasive and persuasive messages, as well as non-sensitive (non-persuasive) messages.
- **Use Cases:** Positive announcements, persuasive pitches, new initiatives.
- **Key Principles:** You deploy all six SUCCES principles: Simple, Unexpected, Concrete, Credible, Emotional, and Stories.

With this consolidated framework, you now understand:

- Neurobiology is the reason messages stick.
- The six SUCCES Principles make messages stick.
- The StoryBrand (SB7) Framework is the guide for using the sixth, Stories Principle, for crafting and conveying persuasive messages.
- The Stickiness level can be set at very low, average, or very high level by using the right Stickiness Principles.

AI Accelerator: The SUCCES & StoryBrand Prompts

Your AI Assistant is the ultimate "Stickiness Coach" and "StoryBrand Guide." Use these prompts to apply the frameworks from this book:

Prompting the SUCCES Principles

Feed your AI Assistant a dry, boring core message and ask it to apply the SUCCES Principles to make it stick.

Prompt: "Function as an editor schooled in the SUCCES model. Here is my core idea: ['We are implementing a new QA process to improve code quality.'] This is boring. Help me make it sticky. Give me: A Simple core message (the 'strategic intent'); An Unexpected hook (a surprising stat or fact about common bugs).; Concrete details to use (instead of 'code quality,' say 'fewer 2 a.m. server-down calls'); Credible proof (a quote from a lead developer); An Emotional angle (the WIIFM: 'pride in our work'); and A mini-Story to tell."

My AI Assistant's 1st draft: "Zero-Panic Deploys"
"Did you know that fixing a bug after production deployment costs 100 times more than fixing it during the design phase? We aren't just losing time; we are paying a 'lazy tax' on every release."

"This isn't about ticking boxes on a checklist. It's about:

- Zero frantic Slack messages from Customer Support at 4:55 PM on a Friday.
- Never having to explain to a client why their data vanished.
- Ending the culture of 'Hotfix Branches' and getting back to 'Feature Branches.'

"We ran this protocol on the Checkout Module pilot last week. Lead Developer Sarah—who usually spends her Tuesdays fighting fires—said, 'This was the first deployment in six months where I didn't keep my laptop open on the train ride home.'"

"We didn't become developers to be digital janitors, cleaning up messes we made yesterday. We became developers to build cool things. This process gives you the freedom to stop fixing and start building again."

"Remember the 'Login Crash' of last November? The War Room was full of pizza boxes, nobody slept for 24 hours, and we lost three major accounts. Now, look at the API team. They adopted this new QA flow two sprints ago. Last Tuesday, they pushed a major update. The result? Silence. No alarms, no panic, just a quiet Slack channel. They went to Happy Hour while the code did exactly what it was supposed to do. That is the future we are building."

Ask yourself: What is the simple core message (strategic intent) and what is the unexpected "Hook"? Where is concrete sensory language used? What makes this message credible, where's the proof? What makes readers feel emotions? What's the narrative part of the message, the story, which makes this message stick?

Prompting the StoryBrand Framework

Use this "Chain-of-Thought" prompt to have your AI Assistant walk you through the 7-step (SB7) framework.

Prompt: "Function as a StoryBrand Certified Guide. [Insert your idea here]. You will now guide me, one step at a time, to fill out the 7-part SB7 framework. Ask me one question at a time.

1. "A Character ...": Start by asking me who the Character or target audience is and what they want.
2. "Has a Problem ...": After I answer, ask me for the External, Internal, and Philosophical problems and offer to draft three examples.
3. "And Meets a Guide ...": Then, ask me how to show Empathy and Authority and offer to draft three examples.
4. "Who Gives Them a Plan ...": Then, ask for a simple 3-step plan and offer to draft a 3-step plan.
5. "And Calls Them to Action...": Then, ask for the direct Call to Action and offer to draft three examples.
6. "That Helps Them Avoid Failure.": Then, ask me what's at stake and offer to draft three examples.
7. "And Ends in a Success": Ask me what the success, "happy ending", looks like and offer to draft three examples.

After we have all 7 parts, assemble them into a complete BrandScript."

CEO's Guide to High-Impact Business Writing

A 4-Step Framework for Leadership Communication. This guide provides a structured approach for executives to improve their own communication and coach their teams to write with clarity, authority, and empathy.

1. **Learn How to Write the Commander's Intent Statement** Before writing a message, you must define your target audience and your desired measurable outcome. This is your "strategic brief".
2. **Learn How to Choose Structure, Style, and Stickiness** Once the core message is clear, analyze your audience and predict how they'll react to the message. Research the issues and collect information and data to understand what your audience wants and to support your desired outcome. Based on your prediction, choose the message type that most likely produces the desired outcome and stays in the audience's mind, if needed.
3. **Learn How to Write and Refine using AI Assistants** Use AI not just to generate text, but to sharpen your thinking and polish your output.
4. **Learn How to Personalize the Message** Use AI not to personalize the message, but to assess and fine tune the final message to minimize the likelihood of producing an undesired outcome.

CHAPTER 10: THE PSYCHOLOGY OF INFLUENCE

In Part I, we built the logical structure of your message. In Part II, we made it "Sticky." But to move a reader from *agreement* to action, you need more than logic, you need **influence.** Robert Cialdini, PhD, the Regents' Professor Emeritus of Psychology and Marketing at Arizona State University and author of the seminal work, *Influence: The Psychology of Persuasion,* introduced the six persuasion principles. They are the "invisible levers" of business writing. While Cialdini wrote the manual on human influence, we are now learning to scale these principles using AI Assistants. When combined with AI, they allow you to engineer for results with scientific precision.

The Principles of Persuasion

Here are the six persuasion principles and how to use them in messaging:

Reciprocity: Give Before You Ask

The human brain is wired to return favors.

In business writing, offer value upfront to create a psychological "indebtedness."

- **Message Types:** Use for crafting Positive Persuasive messages targeting universal audiences and Negative Persuasive Messages targeting Superiors.
- **The Agile Move:** Provide a useful template, a white paper, or a specific insight before your Call to Action.
- **AI Prompt Tip:** "Rewrite this sales email to lead with a valuable industry insight rather than a request for a meeting."

Commitment & Consistency: Leverage Small Wins

People strive to align their current actions with past commitments.

- **Message Types:** Use for crafting Negative Persuasive Messages targeting your Subordinates.
- **The Agile Move:** Start with a "micro-commitment," such as asking for a newsletter sign-up or a simple "yes" to a non-controversial question.
- **AI Prompt Tip:** "Structure this pitch to lead with three easy-to-agree-upon facts about our industry's current challenges."

Social Proof: Use the Power of the Crowd

In uncertainty, people look at others. Use testimonials, data points, and "The Crowd" to build credibility.

- **Message Types:** Use for crafting Positive Persuasive messages targeting universal audiences.
- **The Agile Move:** Use specific numbers ("95% of our users...") rather than vague claims ("Most of our users...").
- **AI Prompt Tip:** "Insert three placeholder slots for specific customer metrics that demonstrate social proof."

Liking: Humanize the Pilot

We are more likely to say "yes" to people we like. Authenticity is the antidote to synthetic text.

- **Message Types:** Use for crafting Negative Persuasive messages targeting external audiences like customers and partners.
- **The Agile Move:** Use conversational language and find common ground. Share a brief "Proof of Life" story.
- **AI Prompt Tip:** "Function as an Editor. Make this report sound more approachable and human while maintaining executive authority."

Authority: Cite the Masters

People defer to expertise. Establish your authority (and your AI Assistant's) by citing data and frameworks.

- **Message Types:** Use for crafting Negative Persuasive Messages targeting your Subordinates and Superiors.
- **The Agile Move:** Cite industry research or established models (like the SUCCES model).
- **AI Prompt Tip:** "Ground this recommendation in the latest McKinsey research on digital transformation."

Scarcity: Create an Urgent Knowledge Gap

We value what is rare. Create a sense of urgency without sounding like a used-car salesman.

- **Message Types:** Use for crafting Negative Persuasive messages targeting external audiences like customers and partners.
- **The Agile Move:** Highlight time-sensitive opportunities or exclusive "Pilot Group" access.
- **AI Prompt Tip:** "Refine this invitation to emphasize that the beta-testing window closes this Friday."

Persuasion Principles for Persuasive Message Types

Message Type **(Target Audience)**	**Persuasion Principles**	**Reasoning**
Positive Persuasive (Universal)	Reciprocity & Social Proof	Lead with value to create indebtedness, then show that others are already seeing results to drive enthusiastic adoption.
Negative Persuasive Internal Down (Subordinates)	Authority & Commitment	Leverage your institutional standing while anchoring the correction in the employee's existing commitment to team goals.
Negative Persuasive Internal Up (Superiors)	Authority & Reciprocity	Cite expert frameworks or data to justify the pivot (Authority) and offer a proactive solution to the bad news (Reciprocity).
External Negative Persuasive (Customers/Partners)	Liking & Scarcity	Use a personal touch to preserve the bond (Liking) and frame the "bad news" as a window to secure exclusive future value (Scarcity).

THE PERSUASION AUDIT

Before you hit send, ask: Which lever am I pulling? If your message has high stakes but contains zero psychological leverage, you are leaving your desired outcome to chance. Instead use the Persuasion Matrix to select the right psychological lever for your Agile Message Strategy.

The Persuasion Matrix

Principle	When to Use	The Agile Move (The "Now What?")
Reciprocity	Lead Generation / Sales	Offer a high-value template or insight before you ask for a meeting.
Commitment	Change Management	Secure a small "Yes" (e.g., newsletter sign-up) to build a path toward a larger mandate.
Social Proof	Building Trust	Use hard metrics ("95% success rate") rather than vague adjectives ("excellent results").
Liking	Relationship Building	Share a brief personal "Proof of Life" story to humanize the digital void.
Authority	Strategy Approval	Ground your claims in established frameworks like the OODA Loop or SUCCES model.
Scarcity	Driving Urgency	Highlight the "Knowledge Gap" or time-sensitive nature of the opportunity.

THE PILOT'S FINAL COMMAND

Precision communication is the weapon; agility is the movement. Use these levers ethically to achieve your Commander's Intent.

CHAPTER 11: THE STYLE TOOLKIT

In the last three chapters, we've focused on "Stickiness", the science of making your message memorable and impactful. Now, we turn to Style.

If structure is the "what," and stickiness is the "impact," style is the "how." It's the collection of choices in tone, word choice, and phrasing that give your message its unique feel. For example, an "urgent" message feels different from a "reassuring" one, even if the core information is the same.

The framework defines style not as a vague "voice," but as a set of deliberate, strategic choices. We can map these choices into three primary "spectrums of style," which we use to create four core styles.

At the end of Part II, we'll know how to use these four style combinations with the three structural patterns and the six stickiness principles.

The 3 Spectrums of Style

Every message you write can be placed on these three spectrums. Your choices here are just as important as your structural choice.

- **The Authority Spectrum (Forceful vs. Passive)** Forceful style uses the active voice, clear commands, and confident language. Passive style uses passive voice, suggestions, and cautious phrasing.
- **The Relationship Spectrum (Personal vs. Impersonal)** Personal style uses pronouns like "I," "we," and "you" to connect directly with the reader. It's conversational. Impersonal style avoids personal pronouns in favor of objective, third-person, or institutional language.
- **The Engagement Spectrum (Colorful vs. Colorless)** Colorful style uses vivid adjectives, strong verbs, analogies, and engaging language to create excitement and paint a picture. Colorless style uses factual, objective, and plain language. It is precise and unadorned.

These three spectrums of style are your fundamental tools, the elements you, as the Writer, will use. We'll learn how to combine these spectrums to create the four powerful core styles for any business situation.

The 4 Core Style Combinations

We defined the three core spectrums of style:

- Authority Spectrum (Forceful/Passive),
- Relationship Spectrum (Personal/Impersonal), and
- Engagement Spectrum (Colorful/Colorless).

Now, we move from theory to practice.

Your job as an Analyst is to combine these ingredients to build a complete message strategy. By combining these spectrums, we can create the distinct, powerful styles you defined for the most common business situations.

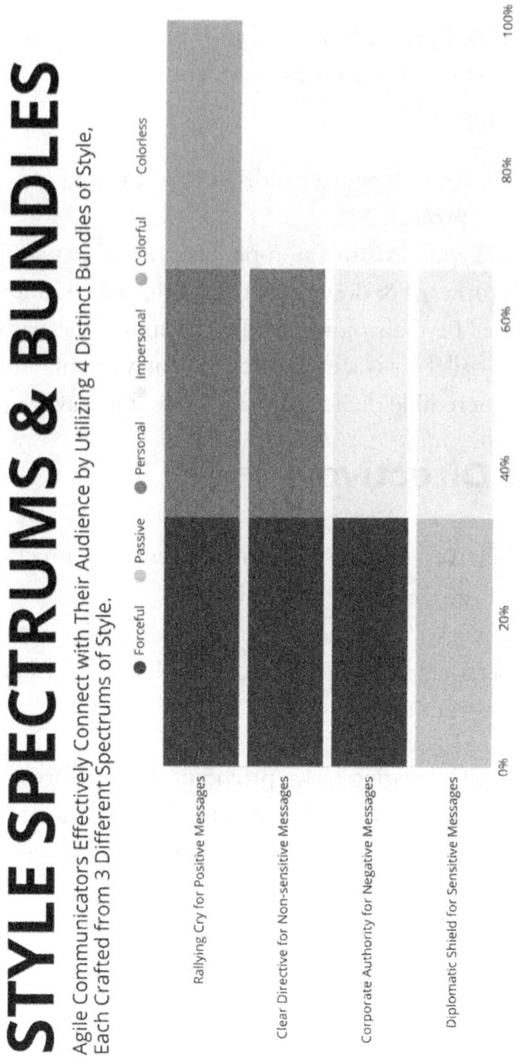
STYLE SPECTRUMS & BUNDLES
Agile Communicators Effectively Connect with Their Audience by Utilizing 4 Distinct Bundles of Style, Each Crafted from 3 Different Spectrums of Style.
Forceful
Passive
Personal
Impersonal
Colorful
Colorless
Rallying Cry for Positive Messages
Clear Directive for Non-sensitive Messages
Corporate Authority for Negative Messages
Diplomatic Shield for Sensitive Messages
0%
20%
40%
60%
80%
100%

The Rallying Cry

The "Rallying Cry" style is a combination of Forceful, Personal, and Colorful ends of the three spectrums of style.

This style inspires me. It's used to motivate a team, celebrate a big win, or launch a new initiative. It combines confident language, a human connection, and vivid, exciting words.

- Use Case: Announcing a major success, kicking off a new product, service, or project.
- Message Types: Positive non-persuasive and persuasive messages for internal (upward & downward) and external communication.
- Example: "I am absolutely thrilled to announce that we've shattered our Q3 goal! This is a monumental achievement, and it's all because of your incredible dedication. Let's ride this wave!"

The Clear Directive

The "Clear Directive" style is a combination of Forceful, Personal, and Colorless ends of the three spectrums of style.

This is the workhorse of daily management. It's professional, efficient, and clear. It's personal ("I," "you") but avoids colorful language to remain focused on the instruction.

- Use Case: Delegating tasks, providing straightforward updates, setting deadlines, delivering information, for example.
- Message Types: Non-sensitive non-persuasive messages for upward and downward as well as internal and external communication.
- Example: "Hi Team, please submit your Q3 expense reports by this Friday. I've attached the official guidelines. Let me know if you have any questions."

The Diplomatic Shield

The "Diplomatic Shield" style is a combination of Passive, Impersonal, and Colorless ends of the three spectrums of style.

This is the style you use to communicate carefully, objectively, and neutrally. It's used to de-escalate conflict, deliver sensitive news, or communicate with a hostile audience. It removes all personal emotion and blame.

- Use Case: Responding to an angry customer, rejecting a vendor, delivering bad news to a superior.
- Message Types: Internal negative persuasive and non-persuasive messages targeting your superiors (upward) and external negative persuasive and non-persuasive messages targeting your customers, business partners, suppliers, or other (external) stakeholders.
- Example: "Thank you for your application. After careful consideration, the decision has been made to move forward with another candidate. This decision was based on a variety of factors."

The Corporate Authority

The "Corporate Authority" style is a combination of somewhat Forceful, Impersonal, and Colorless ends of the three spectrums of style.

This is the formal, "Voice of the Company." It is firm, objective, and official. It is not a person speaking, but the institution. It's used for announcements that are final and not up for debate.

- Use Case: Announcing a new company-wide policy, departmental restructuring, or legal statements.
- Message Types: Negative non-persuasive (non-negotiable) messages targeting your subordinates (downward).
- Example: "Effective November 1st, the operations department will be restructured to align with strategic priorities. This is a necessary step to ensure long-term organizational health."

The Style Completes Your Agile Message Strategy

Your Message Strategy is now almost complete. Now you choose the message structure, style and stickiness combination based on the audience analysis results.

By consciously choosing structure, stickiness, and style, you move from being a simple writer to being a true agile communicator. But our work isn't quite done. Once the message strategy is set, it must be drafted, refined, and personalized.

The Agile Message Strategy Matrix

<table>
<tr><th>Message Type
Target Audience</th><th>Message Structure</th><th>Message Style</th><th>Stickiness Principles</th><th>Persuasiveness Principles</th></tr>
<tr><td>Positive Message
Universal Audiences</td><td rowspan="4">Direct</td><td rowspan="2">Rallying Cry</td><td rowspan="3">SUCCES</td><td>N/A</td></tr>
<tr><td>Positive Persuasive Message
Universal Audiences</td><td>Reciprocity
Social Proof</td></tr>
<tr><td>Non-sensitive Message
Universal Audiences</td><td>Clear Directive</td><td>N/A</td></tr>
<tr><td>Negative Message
Internal Stakeholders: Subordinates</td><td rowspan="2">Corporate Authority</td><td rowspan="2">Simple
Credible
Concrete</td><td>N/A</td></tr>
<tr><td>Negative Persuasive Message
Internal Stakeholders: Subordinates</td><td rowspan="3">Hybrid</td><td>Authority
Commitment</td></tr>
<tr><td>Negative Message
Internal Stakeholders: Superiors</td><td rowspan="4">Diplomatic Shield</td><td>Simple
Credible</td><td>Authority
Reciprocity</td></tr>
<tr><td>Negative Persuasive Message
Internal Stakeholders: Superiors</td><td>Simple
Credible
Concrete</td><td>N/A</td></tr>
<tr><td>Negative Message
External Stakeholders</td><td rowspan="2">Indirect</td><td>Simple
Credible</td><td>Liking
Scarcity</td></tr>
<tr><td>Negative Persuasive Message
External Stakeholders</td><td>Simple
Credible
Concrete</td><td>N/A</td></tr>
</table>

CHAPTER 12: THE CRAFT OF REFINING MESSAGES

Before we start drafting and refining messages, we must first diagnose the problem. Why is business writing so bad?

It's not an accident. It's learned behavior, and it's reinforced by corporate culture. It has become a massive, quantifiable business problem. As researcher Josh Bernoff found in his study for *Harvard Business Review*, this "productivity-draining blather" is a hidden source of friction. He surveyed 547 businesspeople and found that 81% agree that poorly written material wastes a lot of their time, but how much time?

Bernoff's data shows that professionals spend an **average of 25.5 hours per week** reading for work. About one third of this is reading emails. The majority said that what they read is frequently ineffective because it's "too long, poorly organized, unclear, filled with jargon, and imprecise." This "fuzzy writing" doesn't just waste time; as Bernoff notes, it "allows fuzzy thinking." This is the cycle of "productivity-draining blather":

Leaders, in a rush, send fragmented, unclear, "first-draft emails." Employees receive this "flabby writing," which wastes their time (the 25.5 hours/week) as they try to decipher it. This culture reinforces bad habits, and the "whole organization drowns." Even worse, this habit is taught.

As writer David Silverman notes, our educational system "rewards length over clarity." This bad habit follows us to the corporate world, where we use "expensive-sounding words" like "utilize" or "actionize" when "use" or "do" would be clearer and we feel we are "paid by the word." And you pay per word if you decide to outsource copywriting to a freelance copywriter. For example, the American Writers & Artists Inc. (AWAI) states that the average freelance copywriting rate for 2025 is approximately $0.70 per word. This is why concision is not just a writing skill; it is a leadership imperative.

Refining your message is not just an editing task; it is an act of "forcing fuzzy thinking into clarity" and a hallmark of leadership. In business communication, brevity respects your reader's time and attention.

Brevity is a sign of respect.

How To Tighten and Brighten

A shorter, clearer message is not just easier to read, it's more likely to be read in the first place. This concept is known as "processing fluency." Processing fluency builds credibility. Simple messages feel true. Fluff, "bizspeak," and long-winded sentences create friction, causing your reader's brain to work harder and diminishing your message's impact.

How To Eliminate Corporate Jargon

The first step is to eliminate what Bryan Garner calls the "Blacklist", words that are corporate jargon and add no real value. Instead of: "We must leverage our core competencies to actionize our learnings moving forward." Say: "We must use our skills to apply what we learned." Words to Cut: Leverage, actionize, learnings, utilize, impact (as a verb), synergize, core competency, moving forward, circle back, etc.

How To Kill Nominalizations

How To Kill "-ion" Words (Nominalizations)? Nominalizations are verbs and adjectives that have been turned into bulky nouns, often ending in "-ion," "-ment," or "-ance." Turning them back into verbs makes your writing more direct and powerful. Instead of: "We will make a determination..." Say: "We will determine..." Instead of: "It is our expectation that..." Say: "We expect..." Instead of: "The implementation of the plan..." Say: "We implemented the plan..."

How To Replace Verbs with Stronger Verbs

The strongest word in a sentence is the verb. Don't waste it. Avoid weak "be" verbs (is, are, was, were) and bland verbs (have, make, do, give) when a more precise one exists. Instead of: "We are having a meeting to give consideration to the problem." Say: "We are meeting to consider the problem." Instead of: "The new policy is a major change." Say: "The new policy changes the company."

How To Cut Prepositional Clutter

Prepositional phrases (of the..., in the..., for the...) are the barnacles on the hull of your writing. They slow you down. Find them and cut them. Instead of: "The decision of the manager for the project..." Say: "The project manager decided..." Instead of: "The memo is in regard to the new rules for the office." Say: "The memo explains the new office rules."

How To Test for Tone: The Propriety Test

Before you send a sensitive or persuasive message, apply this simple check: "Would you care to take action on the basis of what your own communication presents?" If you, as the reader, are offended by the message, confused, or feel damaged by taking the suggested action, you must restate communication.

How To Find Flaws: The Read It Aloud Test

"Read It Aloud" is a key editing technique to reveal flaws that your eyes skip over. Reading a passage aloud forces your brain to slow down. You will immediately hear clunky sentences, gaps in your argument, awkward phrasing, and poor rhythm that you would otherwise miss.

Refining with AI: The "Ruthless Editor" Prompt

We have discussed the manual craft of refining. But as an Agile Communicator, you don't always have time to hunt for every "zombie noun" yourself. This is where your AI Assistant becomes your most valuable tool—not as a writer, but as a ruthless editor. You can train your AI Assistant to apply the "Tighten & Brighten" principles instantly. Use this specific prompt to turn your AI into a precision editing machine.

The RTF Prompt for "Tighten & Brighten"

(Role) "Function as a ruthless editor." **(Task)** "I am pasting a draft below. Your goal is to improve clarity and brevity without changing the core meaning. Please apply the following rules: **(Task1: Cut the Fluff)** Remove all corporate jargon, words like leverage or synergy, and replace jargon with Plain English. **(Task 2: Kill the Zombies)** Find all nominalizations, nouns ending in -tion, -ment, or -ance, and turn them back into active verbs. **(Task 3: Active Voice)** Change all passive voice sentences to active. **(Task 4: Brevity)** Cut the word count by at least 20%." **(Format)** "Output two versions:**(Format: Version 1)** A tracked changes list of what you just fixed. **(Format: Version 2)** and the final, polished draft."

When you ask for Version 1, you force your AI Assistant to show its work, which helps you learn *why* the changes were made. Over time, this trains *your* brain to spot these errors before you even type them.

The "Tighten & Brighten" Checklist

Before you hit send on any high-stakes message, run it through this filter:

The "Of" Monster Filter (Tighten)

- **The Check**: Search for the words "of the" and "in the."
- **The Fix:** Delete them. Flip the sentence. Instead of: "The manager of the project in the marketing department..." Say: "The Marketing Project Manager..."

The "Zombie" Nouns Filter (Tighten)

- **The Check:** Search for words ending in -tion, -ment, and -ance. These are nominalizations—verbs that have been killed and turned into heavy nouns.
- **The Fix:** Turn them back into verbs. Instead of: "We made a determination to prioritize the implementation..." Say: "We determined to implement..."

The "Be-Verb" Ban Filter (Brighten)

- **The Check:** Search for is, are, was, and were.
- **The Fix:** Replace them with a verb that does actual work. Instead of: "This is impactful for our Q3 results." Say: "This boosts our Q3 results."

The "Adverb" Slash Filter (Brighten)

- **The Check:** Search for words ending in -ly (really, very, hopefully).
- **The Fix:** Delete them. If the verb is strong enough, it doesn't need a prop. Instead of: "We really need to move quickly." Say: "We must sprint."

CHAPTER 13: CONCLUSION TO PART II

You have now mastered the human-led strategy. In Part I, you learned how to think like an Analyst, defining your Commander's Intent and choosing the right Structure. In Part II, you learned the Craft of the Writer and Editor. You learned that logic alone is not enough; a message must stick, it must have a voice, and it must be refined with ruthless precision.

The Craft of the Agile Communicator

You have now built the complete "Human Strategy." You have the "what" (Structure) and the "how" (Style & Stickiness).

The Readiness Check

Before you turn the page to Part III and activate your AI Assistant, you must pass this final check. Do not proceed until you can answer "Yes" to these three questions:

The Impact Check: Is it Sticky?

- Have you chosen the specific principles: Simple, Unexpected, Concrete, Credible, Emotional, and Stories that make your message unforgettable?
- Does your message have a hook?

The Voice Check: Is Style Strategic?

- Have you consciously chosen your tone? Is this a "Rallying Cry" to inspire, or a "Diplomatic Shield" to protect?
- Or are you just writing in your default voice?

The Polish Check: Is it Tight and Bright?

- Have you run the "Tighten & Brighten" checklist?
- Have you killed the zombie nouns and slashed the adverbs? Is every word fighting for its life?

If you can answer "Yes," you are ready.

You have the strategy. You have the craft. Now, let's add speed.

Turn the page to Part III: The AI-Powered Workflow.

Messaging Made Agile

Strategy First, AI Second

Part III: The AI-Powered Workflow

Jorma Manninen

BUSINESS MADE AGILE
WWW.BUSINESSMADEAGILE.COM

PART III EXECUTIVE SUMMARY: THE ENGINE OF SPEED

THE BOTTOM LINE

AI is a high-performance engine, not a magic wand. If you don't know how to steer it, it will drive your reputation off a cliff. Part III provides the protocol for human-led, AI-accelerated messaging. To lead in 2026, you must stop being a Passenger who accepts "Workslop" and start being a Pilot who commands clarity.

KEY TAKEAWAYS

The Prompt Menu AI is like a brilliant but literal intern. Choose the right instruction framework for the task:

- **CO-STAR**: For high-stakes strategy and quality.
- **RTF** (Role, Task, Format): For routine speed.
- **Chain-of-Thought:** To force the AI to "think step-by-step" through complex logic.

The Core AI Workflow Never skip a step in the assembly line:

- **Step Zero (Human Strategy):** Define outcome and audience before opening a chatbot.
- **Step One (Prompt):** Translate strategy into machine instructions.
- **Step Two (Refine):** Guide the AI to "tighten and brighten" its own draft.
- **Step Three (Personalize):** The non-negotiable human touch. Add "Proof of Life" context that proves a person wrote the message.

The Transparency Strategy Authenticity is your most valued asset.

- **Disclose AI use** for process-driven tasks (meeting notes, formal reports).
- **Never use AI** for sensitive human interactions (condolences, personal feedback).
- The Wade Test: Remember that long-tenured employees can spot "synthetic leadership" nearly 60% of the time.

THE PILOT'S PRE-FLIGHT CHECKLIST

- Have I completed Step Zero (Human Strategy)?
- Did I choose the correct prompt framework (CO-STAR or RTF)?
- Have I manually verified every data point and math calculation?
- Did I add a "Proof of Life" element to the final version?

PRO-TIP: THE MATH AUDIT

AI models are text predictors, not calculators. They "guess" the sound of a number rather than calculating it. Never trust an AI with a budget, a metric, or a schedule without a manual re-calculation. One decimal error in a memo can destroy your credibility with a CFO.

CHAPTER 14: INTRODUCTION TO PART III

You have the Strategy (Part I). You have the Craft (Part II). Now it is time to add AI to speed up writing and editing.

The AI-Powered Workflow

We are entering the most technical section of this book. We will cover tools, prompts, workflows, and verification methods. But before we touch a single piece of software, we must set the rules of engagement. AI is not a magic wand. It is like a high-performance race car. If you don't know how to steer it, it will drive you off a cliff.

The Pilot vs. The Passenger

In the age of AI, there are only two types of leaders:

- **The Passengers:** They are "low agency." They type "write an email" and accept whatever generic, robotic text AI spits out. They are creating "Workslop." They are losing authority.

- **The Pilots:** They are "high agency." They use AI to extend their capabilities, not replace their judgment. They set the course, check the instruments, and land the plane.

You are the Pilot.

Your Mission

In Part III, you will master the specific skills required to command this engine. You will not just "use" AI; you will integrate it into a professional workflow:

You will Choose Your Co-Pilot (Chapter 14) You will stop being overwhelmed by the thousands of new tools. You will learn to select the right AI Assistant for your specific role, whether you are a CEO needing a writer or a manager needing an editor.

You will Give Clear Orders (Chapter 15) You will stop typing lazy requests. You will master Prompt Engineering Frameworks like CO-STAR and Chain-of-Thought to force the AI to think at your level.

You will Trust the Protocol (Chapter 16) You will adopt the Core AI Workflow (Strategy - Prompt - Refine - Personalize). This is your safety checklist. It ensures that you never send a hallucination or a robotic message.

You will Know Your Speed (Chapter 17) You will learn to accelerate. You will use AI for Speed to clear your inbox, AI for Influence to brainstorm campaigns, and AI for Nuance to safeguard sensitive news.

You will Own the Flight (Chapter 18) Finally, you will master the Transparency Strategy. You will learn the "Wade Test" and how to protect your authenticity in a world flooded with synthetic text.

The aircraft is ready. The runway is clear. Let's take control.

CHAPTER 15: HOW TO CHOOSE THE RIGHT AI ASSISTANT

In the two parts of this book, you built the complete "Agile Message Strategy." You mastered the human-led skills: Commander's Intent, Audience Analysis, and Message Structure. Now, we add **the AI accelerator.**

We are moving from the human-led process to the **AI-accelerated workflow.** In this new model, you are still the Leader, but you now have a team of tireless, lightning-fast AI Assistants. But "AI" is a vague term. Using it is like saying you're "using the internet." To be an agile communicator, you must be a sophisticated user. That means knowing which *Assistant* to use for which *job.*

This chapter is your guide to the AI landscape, helping you choose the right Co-Pilots, the AI Assistants, for your specific mission.

The AI Landscape: A Strategic Breakdown

The AI world moves fast, but the "types" of Assistants remain stable. Don't get distracted by the thousands of new apps launching every week. You only need to understand these four categories:

The Four AI Categories

Category	What it is	Best Use Case
AI Engines / Platforms The Foundational Models	The massive "brains" that power everything: GPT-4, Gemini, and Claude, for example.	You rarely use these directly. They are the power plant behind the tools you use.
AI Chatbots The Creative Partner	A conversational interface where you talk to a model: ChatGPT, Gemini Advanced, for example.	**Strategy & Brainstorming** Use for drafting "Rallying Cry" speeches, analyzing complex problems, or generating creative ideas, for example.
Embedded AI Assistants The Workflow Accelerator	AI built directly into your email or docs: Copilot for Microsoft 365, Gemini for Google Workspace, for example.	**Speed & Routine** Use for summarizing long email threads, drafting quick replies, or polishing a report without leaving the tab, for example.
Domain Specific Assistants The Specialists	Tools fine-tuned for a specific job: Marketing (Jasper), legal (Harvey), for example.	**Scale & Compliance** Use when you need 100 on-brand blog posts or a legally compliant contract review, for example.

How You Should Use AI

The role of a CEO or senior executive regarding AI has shifted from "overseeing a tech project" to "orchestrating a new operating model." Leaders are now expected to be both the **Chief Visionary** and the **Primary User** of AI to drive a data-first culture. Here is how CEOs and senior executives should strategically and personally use AI.

Personal Productivity & Decision Support: Executives should use AI as a "force multiplier" for their own time, which is organizations' most expensive resource.

- **Synthetic Thought Partner:** Use LLMs to "red team" your own strategy. Ask the AI to find flaws in your expansion plan or to simulate skeptical board members' questions.
- **Information Synthesis:** Instead of reading 50-page briefing docs, use AI to summarize key risks, opportunities, and "asks" from internal reports.
- **Cognitive Offloading:** Use AI meeting assistants to capture "hidden" insights from meetings, ensuring follow-ups are automated and context isn't lost between back-to-back sessions.
- **High-Speed Communication:** Use AI to draft the first version of messages. This allows you to spend your time and energy refining and personalizing your messages rather than staring at a blank page.

Strategic Stewardship: The CEO's job isn't to code; it's to ensure AI investments align with the "North Star" of the company. Identify the "Why" Before the "How" Don't implement AI for the sake of it.

Focus on three things:

- **Efficiency:** Automating the mundane (e.g., back-office processing).
- **Experience:** Improving customer or employee interactions.
- **Expansion:** Creating new revenue streams or business models that were impossible without AI.

Shift to "Agentic AI" in 2025 Last year was the year of AI Agents. Unlike simple chatbots, agents can plan and execute multi-step tasks. Executives should be looking for where agents can function as "digital teammates" in departments like Supply Chain or Customer Success to manage 15–20% of routine decision-making autonomously.

Cultural & Ethical Leadership: The adoption of AI fails more often due to culture than technology. Executives must lead the "Human-AI" transition.

- **Upskilling, Not Just Replacing:** Communicate clearly that AI is meant to "move people up the value chain." Invest in training so employees feel they are being upgraded, not phased out.
- **Responsible AI Frameworks:** Mandate a "Human-in-the-loop" policy for high-stakes decisions. Establish an AI Ethics Board to oversee data privacy and bias, ensuring the company's reputation is protected.
- **Psychological Safety:** Encourage a "Test-Experiment-Learn" mindset. If teams are afraid to fail with AI, they will never find breakthroughs.

Operational Oversight: To ensure AI delivers ROI, senior leaders should monitor these four pillars:

- **Data Quality:** Treat data as a balance-sheet asset. If data is siloed or "dirty," AI is useless.
- **Talent:** Bridge the gap between "Thinkers" (Strategy), "Builders" (Tech), and "Value Creators" (Product).
- **Key Performance Indicators:** Move beyond traditional ROI. Measure AI's impact on agility, speed-to-market, and risk tolerance.
- **Scalability:** Stop "Pilot Purgatory." If a pilot works, give it the budget and mandate to scale enterprise-wide immediately.

Key Mindset Shift for 2026: The CEO of 2026 doesn't just manage people; they manage a hybrid workforce of humans and AI agents. Your competitive advantage is no longer just your product; it's the speed at which your organization learns and adapts using AI.

Role-Specific AI Stacks

An AI stack is the complete collection of tools, technologies, and frameworks that work together to build, train, deploy, and manage artificial intelligence applications. It provides the structured foundation, from core infrastructure to the end-user interface, which enables the creation and scaling of AI solutions.

"Which AI Assistant should you use? It depends on your primary job. Here are my recommended "Starter AI Stacks" to get you from zero to agile immediately.

The AI Stack for CEOs & Senior Executives

- **Primary Goal:** Strategy, Synthesis, and High-Stakes Communication.
- **Premium Chatbot:** Gemini Advanced, ChatGPT Plus, for example. You need the smartest model available for confidential brainstorming and drafting thought leadership.
- **Embedded Assistant:** MS Copilot, Google Gemini, for example: You use this to summarize the 50-email thread before you reply.

Use Chatbots for thinking.
Use the Embedded Assistants for speed.

The Manager's AI Stack

- **Primary Goal:** Team Coordination, Feedback, and Reporting.
- **Embedded Assistant:** This is your workhorse. Use it to draft updates, polish feedback, and turn bullet points into memos.
- **Meeting Intelligence**: Otter.ai, Fireflies, Fathom, for example A tool that records and summarizes meetings automatically. This saves you hours of notetaking and ensures "Commanders Intent" is captured.

The Business Owner's AI Stack

- **Primary Goal:** Everything (Marketing, Sales, Ops).
- **Premium Chatbot:** This is your VP of Marketing, Sales, and Ops in one. Use it to write business plans, draft ad copy, and respond to customer reviews.
- **Visual AI**: Nano Banana, Midjourney. DALL-E, for example. Use this to create professional assets without hiring a designer for every small post.

The Security Check: The Leader's Non-Negotiable

Before you sign up for any tool, you must pass this security check. As a leader, you deal with sensitive data. You cannot afford a leak.

Never use a free AI tool for sensitive data unless you have opted out of training.

- **Free Tools:** Often "pay" for themselves by using your data to train their models. Anything you type becomes part of the public brain.
- **Enterprise/Paid Tools:** Typically offer "commercial data protection," meaning your data stays private and is never used for training the AI.

Your Action: Check your settings today. If you are using a free version for work, upgrade to the Enterprise/Team version immediately. If you can't afford to pay, then *explicitly* opt out of training the free AI tool. The cost of a paid subscription is a fraction of the cost of a data breach.

Visuals: The Ultimate "Concrete" Principle

An agile communicator knows that text isn't always the best way to stick. The "Concrete" and "Emotional" principles often work better with images.

- **AI Image Generation:** Use tools to create custom "Hero Images" for your presentations instead of boring stock photos.
- **Prompt Idea:** "Create a photo-realistic image of a chess piece, the knight, on a circuit board to illustrate the Strategy First, AI Second framework.'"

Forget stock photos, they are forgettable.

You have chosen your Assistant. Now, you must learn to speak its language: "Machine English.".

In the next chapter, we will master the art of **Prompt Engineering.**

CHAPTER 16: PROMPT ENGINEERING FRAMEWORKS

In Chapter 14, you chose your Co-Pilot, your AI Assistant. Now, you must learn to give it orders. But you must first function as the Leader and use your brain to define:

- **Desired Outcome:** What is my business goal (strategic intent) and measurable outcome, result, or reaction?
- **Target Audience:** Who is my audience and how will they react to my core message?
- **Message Type:** What's the right structure for my message? What's the target "stickiness" level and which stickiness principles should I use? What's the right style combination?
- **Communication Channels:** What is the right channel or channels for delivering the message to the audience? Where are they searching for information? What channels do they use for reading, listening, and watching messages?

- **Success Measurement:** What does success look like? How should I measure the actual outcome against my desired outcome? What are my success criteria?

Only after you have the answers to these questions are you ready to prompt.

Prompting is the single most important AI skill for leaders. A prompt is simply an instruction that defines your message strategy for your AI Assistant. A bad prompt will produce bad results even if you use great AI Assistants. Average ones can produce magic if you know how to create a great prompt.

Most leaders fail with AI because they treat it like a search engine. They type vague requests like "Write an email" and get vague results. To become an Agile Communicator, you must treat your AI Assistant like a brilliant but literal intern. It needs context, constraints, and clear instructions.

This chapter gives you the specific frameworks to turn your strategy into expert-level prompts.

The Executive Decision Matrix

There is no single "best" framework for CEOs or senior executives, but there is a best framework for the specific task at hand. In 2026, successful executives use these frameworks like golf bags to select the right club (framework) based on the complexity of the decision. Here is the executive comparison of the top five frameworks. If you're unsure which to use, follow this hierarchy:

- Is it for a high-level audience? Use CO-STAR for strategy.
- Is it a simple fix? Use RTF for speed.
- Is it a strategic project? Use AIM for analysis.
- Does AI generated text sound too "robotic"? Use Few-Shot for style.
- Does AI get the logic wrong? Use Chain of Thought for thinking.

CO-STAR: Use it for high-stakes emails and outputs like board reports, public facing speeches, and persuasive campaigns. Its core focus is precision, and it has high complexity.

RTF: Use it for quick operational delegating, updates, admin tasks, and internal memos. Its core focus is efficiency, and it has low complexity.

AIM: Use it for high level alignment, refining, and fixing existing drafts. Its core focus is strategy, and it has medium complexity.

Few-Shot: Use it for matching your brand voice and specific formatting. Its core focus is consistency, and it has variable complexity.

Chain of Thought (CoT): Use it for solving complex problems, analyzing data, or testing ideas. Its core focus is logic, and it has high complexity.

CO-STAR for Strategy

CO-STAR is **the best all-around framework** to get a high-quality first draft from Large Language Models (LLMs) like Chat GPT, Claude and Gemini.

Use it when the outcome matters or when the audience and tone are critical such as a public-facing speech, a sensitive HR memo, or a branding strategy.

The Six Pillars of CO-STAR

The CO-STAR Framework organizes a prompt into six key pillars.

- **Context:** Who are you? Who is the audience? What is the background?
- **Objective:** What is the desired outcome, this message must achieve?
- **Style:** What is the desired style?
- **Tone:** What is the emotional tone? "Formal," "Urgent," "Empathetic," etc.
- **Action:** What is the specific action the reader should take?
- **Response:** What format? "A 3-paragraph email," "a 500-word memo."

By following this structure, you provide the AI with the "blueprint" it needs to understand not just what to do, but how and for whom. It forces you to provide your AI Assistant with all the critical strategic elements it needs.

An Example of the CO-STAR Prompt

"(C) I am a manager. I am writing to my team of 10 sales reps, who are feeling overworked. (O) The objective is to get them to enthusiastically sign up for a new, optional AI training session. (S) The style is a "Rallying Cry": personal, forceful, and colorful. (T) The tone is exciting, empathetic, and focused on benefits for them. (A) The action is to click a link to sign up for the first session by EOD Thursday. (R) The response should be a short, compelling email draft."

The CO-STAR Framework Eliminates Guesswork.

Most "bad" AI outputs happen because the model is guessing the context or the audience. CO-STAR eliminates guesswork. It is particularly useful for CEOs, senior executives, and top-tier managers because it mirrors the way you would brief a high-level *human* assistant.

RTF for Speed

RTF is a simplified prompting framework designed to be the "quick and dirty" version of CO-STAR. While CO-STAR is great for complex, high-stakes tasks, RTF is the go-to for daily operational efficiency.

Use it for internal, routine tasks where you don't need to specify a complex tone or target a specific external audience. It's faster to type and usually sufficient for 80% of executive work.

The Three Pillars of RTF

The RTF Framework organizes a prompt into three key pillars.

- **Role:** "Function as [INSERT THE ROLE]", for example, "Function as an expert financial analyst," or "Function as a supportive manager"

- **Task:** "Your task is to [INSERT THE TASK]", for example, "Write an email" or "Summarize this document" or "Brainstorm 5 subject lines"
- **Format:** "The format must be [INSERT THE FORMAT]", for example, "A 3-paragraph email" or "A bullet list" or "A professional memo"

Example "RTF" Prompt: "(R) Function as an experienced HR manager. (T) Your task is to draft a company-wide email announcing a new, inconvenient expense reporting process. You must explain why it's necessary (auditor requirements) to get compliance. (F) The format is a professional, 4-paragraph memo using the "Corporate Authority" style."

AIM for Analysis

While CO-STAR is your tool for strategy and RTF is for speed, AIM focuses on the logic and context behind the request.

Use it to process existing documents. You have a quarterly report, a rough draft of a speech, or a resume, and you need your AI Assistant to fix it.

Most AI users fail here because they treat their AI Assistants like a spellchecker. They paste the text and say, "Fix this." Don't fall into this trap. Use the AIM framework when you are in the **Analyst, Writer, or Editor** role and you are providing specific source material that needs to be analyzed, rewritten, or synthesized.

The Three Pillars of AIM

The AIM Framework organizes a prompt into three key pillars.

- **Actor (The Persona):** Instead of just asking for an answer, you tell the AI who it needs to be. This anchors the model's "latent space" to a specific field of expertise, tone, and professional standards. **Executive Tip:** Don't just say "Writer." Say "You are a top-tier McKinsey consultant specializing in digital transformation."
- **Input (The Context & Data):** This is the raw material you provide. It includes the data, background story, constraints, and any "hidden" knowledge the AI wouldn't know otherwise. **Executive Tip:** This is

where you include "proprietary context." For example: "Here is our current Q4 budget and the list of three projects that are currently over-leveraged."

- **Mission (The Objective & Success Criteria):** This is the "why" and the "what." A mission is broader than a simple task; it defines what a successful outcome looks like. **Executive Tip:** Include the intent. Instead of "Summarize this," say "Your mission is to find the three biggest financial risks in this report so I can present them to the Board of Directors tomorrow."

The AIM Framework is often taught as part of "Machine" English; the art of structuring human language so an AI can process it with minimal ambiguity.

"To get expert-level results,
you must learn "Machine" English.

Few-Shot for Style

Few-Shot Prompting is a technique where you give an AI model a handful of examples to show it exactly what you want before you ask it to perform a task.

Use it to get your AI Assistant to adopt your company **brand voice or your own style.** Don't try to describe the style in writing, just show it. Give your AI Assistant 1 to 3 "shots" as examples of what you want, and then you give it the new input.

The "Shot" Spectrum

To understand Few-Shot, it helps to see where it sits on the spectrum of how we talk to AI:

Zero-Shot: You give direct instructions with no examples. For example, you write a prompt: "Write a polite rejection email for a job candidate."

One-Shot: You give exactly one example to show the style. For example, you write a prompt: "Here is how I write: [Example]. Now, write a rejection email for this candidate."

Few-Shot: You give 2 to 5 (or more) examples. This allows the AI to recognize a pattern, tone, and format. For example, you write a prompt: "Example 1: [In/Out], Example 2: [In/Out], Example 3: [In/Out]. Now, do this for [New Input]."

Why Few-Shot is a "Secret Weapon"

While AI models are incredibly smart, they can sometimes be "generic." Few-Shot moves the AI from "generic" to "bespoke." How does it do it?

- **It Solves the "Format" Problem:** If you need data returned to a specific table or a very niche legal format, describing that format in words is hard. Giving three examples of that format is easy. The AI will instantly mimic the structure.
- **It Captures Your Brand Voice:** If you want an AI to write like your brand—not too corporate, but not too casual—Few-Shot is the answer. By providing three earlier blog posts or emails, you "anchor" the AI's creativity to your specific style.
- **It Reduces Hallucinations:** When an AI has examples to look at, it is less likely to wander off into "imaginary" territory. It stays within the logical boundaries set up by your examples.

Pro Tip for 2026: If an AI isn't giving you what you want, don't just "shout" at it with more instructions. Give it three "shots." It is almost always the fastest way to fix a poor output.

A Few Shot Use Case for Executives

The Sentiment Tracker: Imagine you want an AI to categorize hundreds of customer feedback notes into specific internal buckets like [Product Bug], [Pricing Complaint], or [Kudos].

The Few-Shot Prompt would look like this:

- "Categorize the following customer feedback into the correct bucket.
- **Feedback:** The checkout button is broken on mobile. Bucket: [Product Bug]
- **Feedback:** I love the new green color of the app! Bucket: [Kudos]
- **Feedback:** Why did the subscription price double this month? Bucket: [Pricing Complaint]
- **Feedback:** [Insert New Customer Feedback Here] Bucket: "

When Not to Use Few-Shot

- **Simple Facts:** If you just want to know the capital of France, don't waste tokens on examples.
- **Cost/Speed:** Every "shot" you add to a prompt increases the "token count," which means each request costs slightly more and takes a fraction of a second longer to process.
- **Creative Brainstorming:** If you want the AI to give you wild, diverse ideas, examples might limit its imagination.

Chain of Thought for Thinking

Chain of Thought (CoT) is a technique that forces an AI to "think out loud" by breaking a complex problem into a series of logical, intermediate steps before it gives you a final answer. Think of it as the difference between asking close-ended or open-ended questions from your direct reports.

- **Standard Prompting:** "Which is a better investment: Project A or Project B?"
- **Chain of Thought Prompting:** "Analyze Project A and Project B by looking at the IRR, the market risk, and the resource requirements. Think through this step-by-step before giving a recommendation."

Use CoT when you need your AI Assistant to **think and solve complex problems.** Use this for analysis, not just writing. If you have a complex strategic problem, you instruct your AI Assistant with the Magic Phrase: **"Think step-by-step"** to analyze the situation before it gives you the answer. This dramatically improves the quality of its reasoning.

Example CoT Prompt

"I need to pivot our project strategy. Before you write the memo, think step-by-step:

- Analyze the 'Sunk Cost' bias my stakeholders might feel.
- Outline three arguments that reframe this failure as a learning opportunity.
- Recommend the best structure (Direct, Indirect, or Hybrid).
- Then, write the memo based on your analysis.

Try feeding this prompt to your AI Assistant to see its answer.

CoT is a Risk Management Tool

Chain of Thought isn't just a technical trick; it's a risk management tool. There are three benefits of using CoT for thinking:

Auditability: Because the AI shows its steps, you can see where it made a mistake. If it assumes a 5% interest rate in step two, and you know it's 7%, you can catch the error at once.

Reduced "Hallucinations": Your AI Assistant is significantly less likely to make up facts or jump to false conclusions if you force it to follow a step-by-step sequence.

Complex Problem Solving: It allows the AI to manage multi-layered tasks like: "Look at our competitor's new pricing, compare it to our COGS, and suggest a counteroffer that maintains a 20% margin."

When Not to Use CoT

Don't use Chain of Thought for simple tasks. It uses more "tokens" which can increase costs slightly and takes more time to generate.

- Skip it for: Translations, grammar fixes, or simple data retrieval (e.g., "What is our ticker symbol?").
- Mandate it for: Strategy, budgeting, coding, and personnel decisions.

Executive Rule of Thumb

If you wouldn't trust a human's "gut reaction" on a specific topic, don't trust the AI's "Zero-Shot" reaction. Force it into a Chain of Thought.

The Reasoning Models

A new category of AI has appeared. It is called the Reasoning Models or Thinking Models. These models differ from standard AI because they have Chain of Thought (CoT) built into their architecture via reinforcement learning. It is important for CEOs, senior executives, and top-tier managers to understand the shift that has already happened:

- **Feature:** From manually prompted CoT to built-in CoT
- **User Effort:** From "Think step-by-step" to automated thinking.
- **Visibility:** From visible reasoning in the chat to hidden in a bubble.
- **Accuracy:** From good to great. AI self-corrects as it thinks.
- **Cost/Speed:** From standard price and speed.to more expensive and slower speed due to the time AI spends on thinking.

The Primary Reasoning Models

As of late 2025, there were already a few primary models provided with built in CoT as a core feature:

OpenAI: The "o" and "Thinking" Series

- **o1 & o1-mini:** The first generation to introduce "hidden" reasoning tokens.
- **o3 (Standard, Mini, Pro):** The current flagship reasoning models. o3 Pro is widely considered the gold standard for PhD-level science and coding logic.
- **GPT-5 Thinking:** The reasoning-integrated version of the newest frontier model, which generates an explicit, monitorable CoT before answering.

Google: Gemini "Thinking" Models

- **Gemini 2.5 Pro & Flash:** These models introduced "Thinking Budgets," allowing you to set how many tokens the AI can spend on reasoning.
- **Gemini 3 (Pro & Flash):** These models feature a Thinking Level toggle (Minimal, Low, Medium, High), giving you direct control over the "depth" of the AI's logic.

Anthropic: Claude 3.7 & Claude 4

- **Claude 3.7 Sonnet:** The first Claude model to allow "Thinking Time" controls, where the AI can spend up to several minutes "contemplating" a complex coding or legal problem.
- **Claude 4 Opus:** Known for "faithful" reasoning, where the thought process is highly aligned with the final output.

Open-Source & Specialized

- **DeepSeek-R1:** A powerful open-source model that rivaled OpenAI's o1. It is famous for its "Reasoning Content" field, which is accessible via API.
- **Grok 3 (xAI):** Features a "Think Mode" that uses real-time data from X to reason through current events.
- **Kimi K2 Thinking:** A leading model for long-context reasoning, specifically for analyzing thousands of pages of documents.

When to Use Reasoning Models

You should not use these high-reasoning models for everything. They are slower and more expensive because they are effectively "running a marathon" in their head before they give you the answer.

- Use Standard Models for emails, summaries, basic chat, and low stakes brainstorming.
- Use Reasoning Models for financial modeling, legal contract analysis, debugging code, and high-stakes strategic "red-teaming."

The Transparency of Reasoning Models

In 2025, the AI industry was divided into "transparency." While almost all top-tier models now use Chain of Thought (CoT) built-in, they vary significantly in whether they show you the raw logical steps, the "trace", or just a sanitized summary.

For an executive, "full access" is critical for auditing high-stakes decisions, ensuring the AI isn't using biased logic, and verifying that it "understood" your constraints.

The "Full Transparency" Leaders These models provide the raw, unedited stream of reasoning tokens. You see every self-correction, every doubt, and every calculation the AI performs.

- **DeepSeek-R1:** This model is currently the industry standard for transparency. In both its web interface and API, it provides a dedicated reasoning content field. It uses a <think> tag to house its raw logic, which often includes the model literally arguing with itself to find the best answer.
- **Claude 3.7 Sonnet:** Anthropic's 2025 flagship features "Extended Thinking." Unlike OpenAI, Anthropic allows you to see the step-by-step thinking process in a separate UI panel. Through the API, developers can access the full thinking trace, which is essential for "faithful" reasoning; ensuring the final answer follows the logic in the trace.
- **Kimi K2 Thinking:** A prominent model in the 2025 landscape, particularly strong in long-context tasks, Kimi allows users to inspect its intermediate reasoning traces, helping users trace back specific behaviors to the underlying data.
- **OLMo3-Think:** An open-source model from the Allen Institute for AI. It is unique because it allows you to trace intermediate reasoning steps back to the specific training data and decisions that produced them.

The "Summarized" or "Hidden" Models: These models "think" before they speak, but the company deliberately hides or filters the raw thoughts.

OpenAI (o1, o3, GPT-5): OpenAI uses "Hidden Chain of Thought." While the model uses millions of reasoning tokens to solve a problem, those tokens are discarded after the final answer is generated. In the UI, you only see a high-level summary, for example: "Thought for 12 seconds" OpenAI argues this prevents "competitive cloning" i.e., competitors train their models on OpenAI's logic and ensures the thoughts don't violate safety policies.

Gemini 3 (Google): Google provides a "Thinking" toggle. While you can see the model is processing, the full raw trace is generally abstracted into a summary for the user, though enterprise tiers may offer deeper logs for debugging.

The Agile Habit: Iterative Prompting

The first draft is rarely perfect. Agile Communicators iterate by talking back to the machine. Don't rewrite the text manually; prompt the revision. The "Follow-Up" Prompts:

- **For Brevity:** "Too long. Cut the word count by 30%. Keep the main point."
- **For Impact:** "The opening is weak. Give me 5 different 'hooks' that are more surprising."
- **For Clarity:** "Simplify the language. Write it for a smart 12-year-old."

You have the tools. You know the language. Let's look at the **Core Workflow** that ties it all together.

CHAPTER 17: THE CORE AI WORKFLOW

In Chapter 14, you chose your AI Assistant. In Chapter 15, you learned to prompt it. Now, we put it all together into a repeatable system.

This chapter details the single most important process for the modern communicator:

Prompt - Refine - Personalize

This is your "assembly line" for high-impact communication. It combines your human judgment with machine speed. It is the essential loop of human-AI collaboration.

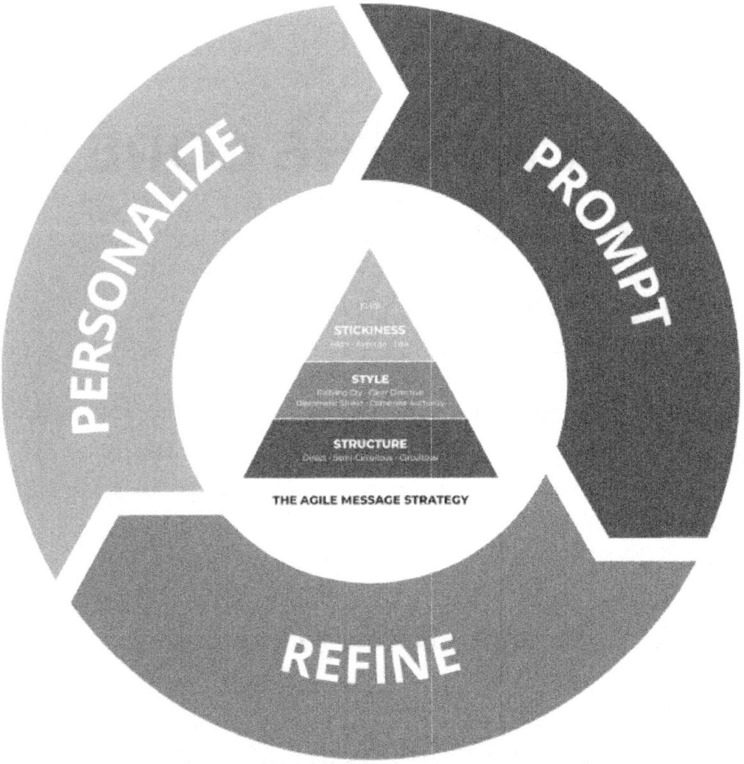

THE CORE AI WORKFLOW

Step Zero: Human Strategy

This is "Step Zero" because it is the prerequisite for all other work. This is the crucial step, and it is the one you must do before you ever open a chatbot window. This is you making critical human-led decisions. You cannot ask an AI Assistant to function as a strategist for you. Before you open a chatbot, you must have a clear brief in your mind (or on paper):

- **Desired Outcome:** What specific action do I want?
- **Target Audience:** How will they react?
- **Message Type:** What structure, stickiness, and style do I need?

If you skip this step, you are just generating noise.

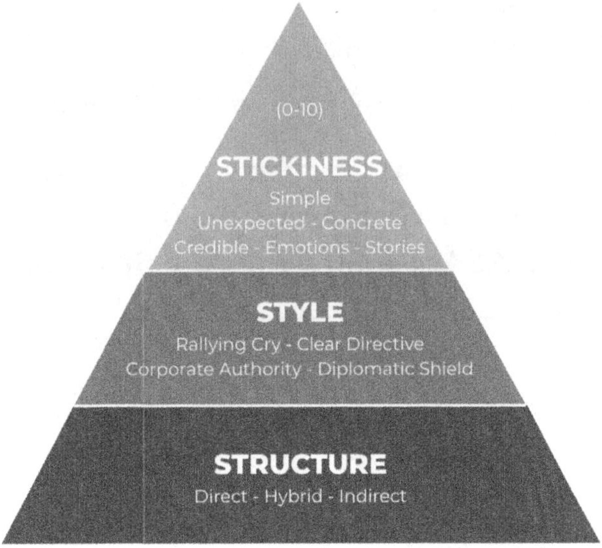

THE AGILE MESSAGE STRATEGY

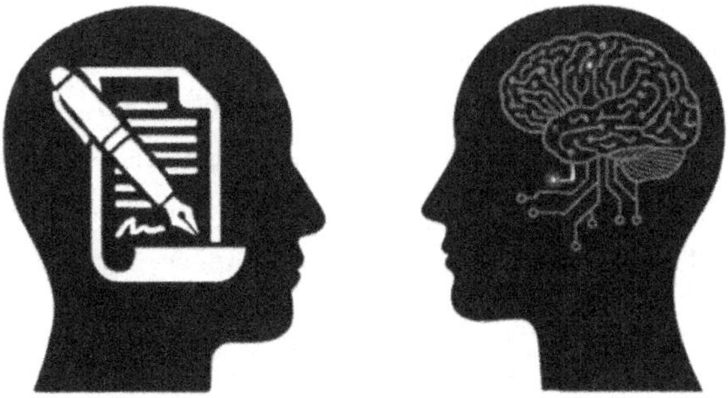

Step One: First Draft

Now, you function as the Writer. Translate your Step Zero strategy into a prompt using one of the frameworks from Chapter 15.

- Input: Your Prompt.
- Output: The AI's First Draft.

Note: The First Draft is almost never the Final Draft. It is raw material.

The Writer inserts the prompt.
The AI Assistant writes the first draft.

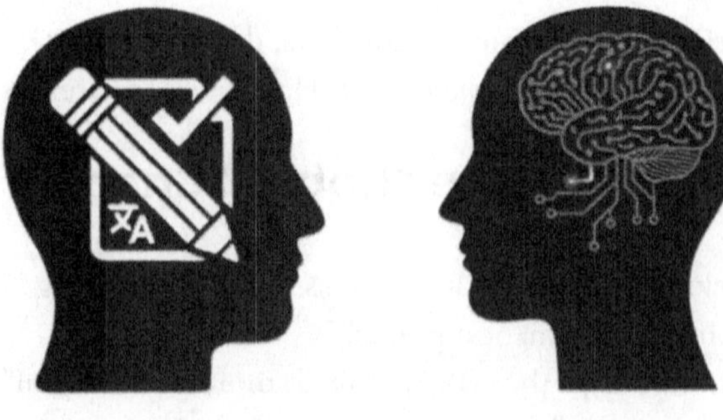

Step Two: Refine

Now, you switch roles. You become the Editor. Your job is not to rewrite the draft manually, but to guide the AI to fix it.

The Editor refines the message with the AI Assistant.

Don't waste time on technical benchmarks. Use this "3-Pass Review" to spot issues fast:

- The Accuracy Pass
- The Tone Pass
- The Strategy Pass

The Accuracy Pass (The "BS" Check)

- Check: Did the AI invent any facts, dates, or names?
- Action: Verify every data point. Hallucinations are the #1 risk.

The Tone Pass (The "Robot" Check)

- Check: Does it sound like a press release? Is it using "happy talk" (too many exclamation points!)?
- Action: Prompt the AI to "make it more professional" or "remove the excitement."

The Strategy Pass (The "Why" Check)

- Check: Does the draft achieve the Desired Outcome from Step Zero?
- Action: If it drifted, prompt: "You lost the main point. Rewrite the opening to focus on [Outcome]."

Advanced Refinement: Debugging the Logic

If the AI keeps giving you bad drafts, stop trying to fix the words. Fix the logic.

- **The Verifier Prompt:** "Ask me three questions that would help you write a better draft."
- **The Chain-of-Thought Prompt:** "Don't write yet. Analyze the audience's objections first. Then write."

Step Three: Personalize

This is the final, non-negotiable step. You must do this manually.

The "Uncanny Valley" Warning: Nothing destroys trust faster than a message that almost sounds human but feels slightly "off." A generic "I hope this email finds you well" screams "I used an AI bot."

The Leader Personalizes the Message.

The Personalization Cheat Sheet

To prove a human wrote this, add one of these "Proof of Life" elements:

Tactic	Example
Specific Context	"I know this deadline is tight, especially with the Q3 review coming up."
Shared Memory	"As we discussed in the elevator yesterday..."
Vulnerability	"I struggled with this decision myself..."
Specific Praise	"I loved how you managed the client's objection in the meeting."
Unique Voice	Use a phrase or idiom you say in real life.

The Harvard Rule: Research shows that employees value effort. When you personalize a message, you signal that you care enough to spend your own time on them.

The Final Accountability Check Before you hit send, ask: *Am I willing to be fired for every word in this email?* If the answer is no, you haven't finished refining.

You are the Leader. The AI is the Assistant. You own the output.

Why is Personalization Non-Negotiable?

In a 2024 study on AI in executive communication, researchers from Harvard Business School found that when employees believed a message was AI-generated, they rated it as "less helpful", even if it was written by a human CEO.

Personalization is not just nice to have. It is the most critical part of the process. Your audience does not just value the information; they value the perceived effort and human connection behind it.

The "Personalize" step is where you re-inject that human effort. It's the step that protects your authenticity and the trust you've built with your audience. Skipping this step is the single biggest risk you can take.

The Accountability Toolkit: Five Verification Methods

Understanding the risk of hallucination is one thing; preventing it is another. In the Air Canada case, the system failed because it was trusted blindly.

As an Agile Communicator, you must never trust blindly. You must verify. To execute "Rule 2: Always Fact-Check," do not just read the text and hope it's correct. Use your AI Assistant to check itself.

Here are five specific "Verification Methods" you can use to force your AI Assistant to criticize its own output and separate intelligence from illusion:

The Assumption Audit AI models often bridge gaps in their knowledge by making plausible-sounding guesses. To catch these hidden risks, ask your AI Assistant to show its work.

- The Prompt: "List every assumption you made in this draft and rank them by your confidence level."
- Value: This exposes the "weak links" in the message that you need to manually verify.

The Source Check Never let an AI state a fact without a citation. If your AI Assistant cannot find a source, the fact is likely a hallucination.

- The Prompt: "Cite two independent sources for each major claim you just made. Include the title, URL, and a one-line quote from the source."
- The Value: This forces the model to ground its creative writing in external reality.

The "Devil's Advocate" (Counterevidence) Confirmation bias is built into AIs; they want to please you. To ensure your argument is robust, force your AI Assistant to argue against it.

- The Prompt: "Find one credible source or argument that disagrees with this message. Explain the dependency or the risk."
- The Value: This prepares you for pushback from your audience and prevents you from sending a message that is easily debunked.

The Math Audit Language models are not calculators. They are text predictors. They often predict the sound of a number rather than the value of a calculation. Never trust an AI with a budget or a metric.

- The Prompt: "Recompute every figure in this message. Show your math or the code you used to calculate it."
- Value: This catches subtle numerical errors that can destroy your credibility with a CFO or a client.

Cross-Model Verification (The "Second Opinion") If the stakes are high (e.g., a crisis response or a legal statement), do not rely on a single "brain." Use one AI to check the work of another.

- The Tactic: Take a draft generated by Gemini and paste it into ChatGPT (or vice-versa).
- The Prompt: "Function as a hostile editor. Critique this text for logical fallacies, potential bias, or factual errors."
- The Value: Different models have different blind spots. By layering them, you create a much tighter safety net than any single model could provide.

By using these five methods, you move from "hoping" your AI Assistant is right to "knowing" it is right. You protect your reputation and ensure that you—not the bot—remain the accountable leader.

CHAPTER 18: AI IN ACTION

In the last chapter, we defined the AI workflow.

"Prompt - Refine - Personalize"

This is your all-purpose process. However, an agile communicator knows how to adapt that workflow based on the desired outcome. Your strategy for a quick status update is completely different from your strategy for a sensitive crisis response.

We can break these outcomes into three main categories:

- AI for Speed (Efficiency)
- AI for Influence (Persuasion)
- AI for Nuance (Safety)

This chapter provides the specific strategies and guardrails for using your AI Assistant in each of these scenarios.

AI for Speed

This is the "autopilot" mode. You are not trying to be inspiring; you are trying to be clear and fast.

- **Goals:** Efficiency, Clarity, and Consistency.
- **Use Cases:** Routine updates, meeting summaries, FAQs, and "drab" admin work.

The Workflow:

- Strategy: Minimal. Use the Direct Structure.
- Prompt: Use RTF (Role, Task, Format) for maximum speed.
- Refine: Check for factual accuracy only.

The "Speed Limit" Rule:

- If you spend more than 2 minutes editing a routine AI draft, you are doing it wrong.
- If the draft is bad, do not rewrite it manually. Write a better prompt. If it's still bad, draft the email yourself. Do not let the tool slow you down.

AI for Influence

This is the "creative partner" mode. You are using AI to brainstorm hooks, find new angles, and structure persuasive arguments.

- **Goals:** Persuasion, Inspiration, and Action.
- **Use Cases:** Sales pitches, "Rallying Cry" team emails, etc.

The Workflow:

- Strategy: Maximum effort. Deep Audience Analysis.
- Prompt: Use CO-STAR and Chain-of-Thought.
- Refine: Iterate. Argue with the AI. "Make it punchier." "Give me a hook."

The OCEAN Framework

AI models default to "average" writing, which kills persuasion. Use the OCEAN Framework to build your prompts and force your AI to have an opinion:

- **Original:** "Give me 3 angles on this topic that no one else is talking about."
- **Concrete:** "Remove all abstract adjectives. Use specific data and examples only."
- **Evident:** "Prove your claim. List 3 bullet points of evidence."
- **Assertive:** "Stop hedging. Pick a side and defend it. Do not say 'it depends'."
- **Narrative:** "Start with a story hook, not a summary."

AI for Nuance

This is the "safety net" mode. You are not using AI to be fast; you are using it to be safe. You use it to remove emotion and ensure your language is neutral.

- **Goals:** Safety, Precision, and Relationship Preservation.
- **Use Cases:** Unwelcome news, apologies, rejections, and high-context cultures.

The Workflow:

- **Strategy:** Use the Indirect Structure, Diplomatic Shield style.
- **Prompt:** "Function as a PR crisis expert. Review this draft for any tone that could be misinterpreted."
- **Personalize:** This is 90% of the work.

The "Apology Rule":

- Never send an AI-generated apology without manually rewriting the first and last sentence.

- AI cannot feel remorse. Its apologies sound hollow ("We regret any inconvenience"). You must inject your own humanity at the start ("I am personally sorry") and the end ("I will fix this").

The SPIKES Protocol for Difficult News

Before your prompt, plan the delivery using this healthcare framework:

- **Setting:** Is email the right channel? (Usually: No).
- **Perception:** What does the audience already know?
- **Invitation:** How much detail do they want?
- **Knowledge:** Deliver the news clearly (no euphemisms).
- **Empathy:** Validate their feelings ("I know this is disappointing").
- **Strategy:** What is the next step?

Use AI to draft the Knowledge and Strategy sections. Write the Empathy section yourself. This is the **highest-risk, highest-reward** use of AI. Here, your AI Assistant is not your accelerator or your creative partner; it is your safety net. Its job is to help you remove emotional, ambiguous, or risky language, providing a safe, neutral "shell" for you to build on.

Your goal is to deliver sensitive or negative news with precision, clarity, and empathy.

In the next chapter, we learn to define the Transparency Strategy for AI

CHAPTER 19: THE TRANSPARENCY STRATEGY

In Chapter 3, you made a high-level decision about transparency. Now, we must execute it. The speed and power of your AI Assistant are useless if the message destroys the trust, you've worked years to build.

Authenticity is the most valued human asset in the age of synthetic text. If your team suspects you are automating your empathy, you lose their loyalty. If they suspect you are hiding your tools, you lose your credibility.

This chapter provides specific scripts, policies, and protocols to protect your reputation.

The Cost of Faking It

The "Wade Test" (The Trust Risk)

Researchers trained AI in the writing style of Wade Foster, CEO of Zapier. They found that employees could spot the "fake Wade" 59% of the time. Long-tenured employees were even better at spotting it.

- **The Lesson:** You cannot fool your team. If you skip the "Personalize" step (Chapter 16), you will be caught. And once caught, every future message you send will be doubted.

The Air Canada Case (The Legal Risk)

A chatbot promised a customer a discount that didn't exist. Air Canada argued the bot was a "separate legal entity." The court disagreed and forced the airline to pay.

- **The Lesson:** You are the Editor-in-Chief. You cannot blame the intern, and you cannot blame the bot. You are 100% liable for every word your AI generates.

The "Competence Penalty" of Laziness

We know that inauthenticity destroys trust, but new research shows it also destroys your reputation. Colleagues who are caught sending lazy, unedited AI content called "Workslop" suffer a severe 'competence penalty.'

Studies show that senders of "Workslop" are viewed by their peers as: Less Creative, Less Capable, and Less Trustworthy.

This is why the 'Personalize' step in our workflow is non-negotiable. It isn't just about making the email sound nice; it's a career-survival skill. When you add your unique voice and strategic intent to a message, you signal to your team that you are a 'Pilot', someone who uses AI with high agency and purpose, not a 'Passenger' who is just using it to avoid work.

WARNING: Don't Create "Workslop"

The Disclosure Scripts

Don't guess how to disclose AI. Use these tested scripts to set the right expectation.

Scenario	The Strategy	The Script (Copy/Paste)
Internal Process Meeting notes	Full Disclosure Show off your efficiency. It models good behavior.	"I used our AI Assistant to summarize the key points from today's meeting. Please review and let me know if I miss anything."
Formal Documents Reports, policies	Professional Disclosure Signal that this is a "first draft" for review.	"This draft was generated with AI assistance to ensure we covered all compliance bases. I have reviewed it, but please check for specific domain accuracy."
Sensitive / Personal Feedback, condolences	Zero Disclosure (Because you shouldn't use it).	[Do not use AI. Write this yourself.]
Creative Brainstorming Campaign Ideas	Collaborative Disclosure.	"I worked with the AI to generate 10 possible angles. Here is the top 3 I selected."

The Accountability Toolkit

To protect yourself from the "Air Canada" fate, you must run every AI draft through this verification check.

The 3-Point Verification Check:

- **The Assumption Audit:** Ask the AI: "List every assumption you made in this draft." (It often guesses dates or budgets).

- **The Source Check:** Ask the AI: "Cite the specific URL or document where you found this fact." (If it can't find it, it hallucinated it).
- **The "Devil's Advocate":** Ask the AI: "What is the strongest argument against this draft?" (This prevents blind spots).

Your Final Move: The AI Policy for Teams

Agility requires shared rules. Don't let your team guess what is allowed. Copy this policy and send it to your team today.

Team Policy: Our Rules for AI Use

- **We are Pilots, not Passengers.** We use AI to think faster, not to avoid thinking. Never copy-paste an AI draft without reading, refining, and verifying it.
- **We Personalize Trust.** We never use AI to write sensitive feedback, apologies, or personal notes. If it requires empathy, it requires a human.
- **We Own the Output.** " The AI wrote it" is not a valid excuse. If you send it, you are responsible for its accuracy, tone, and legality.
- **We Protect Our Data.** Never paste confidential client data or internal strategy into a public, free AI tool. Use only our approved, enterprise-secure tools.

A Practical Standard: To enforce this accountability, require colleagues or editors to suggest at least two meaningful changes per page or message. This ensures a human has truly refined the draft, catching typos and awkward phrasing before it's sent. Ultimately, transparency isn't just about a one-time disclosure. It's about building an Agile Culture where you have clear, shared rules for how your team uses these powerful Assistants. This is how you blend machine speed with the human trust that truly matters.

You now have the complete system. You have the Strategy (Part I). You have the Craft (Part II). You have the Workflow (Part III). Now, let's see exactly what this looks like in the real world. In Part IV, we will open the Agile Message Strategy Casebook.

CHAPTER 20: CONCLUSION TO PART III

You now have the complete system. You have:

- Strategy (Part I),
- Craft (Part II), and
- Workflow (Part III).

Cleared for Takeoff. You have built the engine. In Part III, you moved from human strategy to machine execution. You selected your Co-Pilot, learned the language of Prompt Engineering, and adopted the Core AI Workflow. You also established the Transparency Strategy to protect your most valued asset: trust.

The theory is complete. Now, we are moving to practice. In Part IV, we will open the Agile Message Strategy Casebook. We will walk through 12 real-world scenarios, from celebrating a win to firing a vendor, and show you exactly how to apply every tool in this book. Now, let's see exactly what this looks like in the real world. But before you turn the page, you must confirm your systems are online.

THE PREFLIGHT CHECKLIST

Do not proceed until you check the items on the Pilot's Preflight Checklist:

I – The Co-Pilot Selection

- Have you chosen your specific AI Assistant for your role?
- Do you have the enterprise version to protect your data?

II – The Prompt Engineering

- Do you have the CO-STAR and RTF frameworks saved somewhere accessible?
- Are you ready to stop typing "write an email" and start typing strategic instructions?

III – The AI Workflow

- Have you committed Step Zero?
- Will you refuse to open the chatbot until you have defined your message strategy?

IV – The Transparency Policy

- Have you sent the Team Policy to your direct reports?
- Does everyone know the "rules of the road?"

THE FINAL CHECKLIST

I – The Commander's Intent

- Strategic Intent: Why is the message important?
- Desired Outcome: What is the required action?

II – The Analyst's Blueprint

- Target Audience: What is the predicted reaction?
- Communication Channel: What is the main channel?
- Document Type: What is the document type?
- Structure: What is the structure: Direct, Indirect, or Hybrid?
- Style: What is the style: Rallying Cry, Clear Directive, Corporate Authority, or Diplomatic Shield?

III – The Writer's Craft

- Stickiness: What stickiness principles are in use: Simple, Unexpected, Credible, Concrete, Emotional, or Stories?
- Persuasiveness: What persuasion principles are in use: Reciprocity, Commitment, Social Proof, Liking, Authority, or Scarcity?

IV – The Final Verification

- AI Verification: Did we run the Accuracy, Tone, and Strategy passes?
- Proof of Life: Is my human voice present in the first and last lines?
- Transparency: Should I disclose AI use: Yes / No?

Final Question: Should I send it, refine it, or delete it? Now you can step into the cockpit and take the controls. Start reclaiming your 1,200 hours. Lead the strategy; let AI manage the writing. If you are ready, let's fly.

Turn the page to Part IV: The Agile Message Strategy Casebook.

Messaging Made Agile

Strategy First, AI Second

Part IV: The AI-Message Strategy in Action

PART IV EXECUTIVE SUMMARY: THE CASEBOOK

THE BOTTOM LINE

Part IV is your strategic template library. Strategy is useless without execution; this section provides the "Red/Yellow/Green" blueprint for the 12 most common leadership communication scenarios. Use these examples as your starting point to reclaim 1,200 hours and drive crystalline clarity through your organization.

KEY TAKEAWAYS

The Traffic Light Navigation

- **Green Light (Chapters 22-24):** Positive Non-Persuasive (Celebration), Positive Persuasive (The Pitch), and Non-Sensitive (Directive). Goal: Momentum and clarity.
- **Yellow Light (Chapters 25-28):** Negative Downward (Command/Correction) and Negative Upward (Decline/Pivot). Goal: Changing behavior or plans without losing trust.

- **Red Light (Chapters 29-30):** External Negative (Refusal/Negotiation). Goal: Closure and legal safety while preserving reputation.

The Case Study Framework Each chapter follows a repeatable AI Workflow:

- Strategic Intent: Defined by the Leader.
- Prompt Framework: Usually CO-STAR for high-stakes influence.
- Cultural Context: Specific guidance for Low-Context (explicit) vs. High-Context (implicit) cultures.

THE CASEBOOK CHECKLIST

- Have I identified the "Traffic Light" color and Structure for this situation?
- Am I using the AIDA or StoryBrand "Guide" position in persuasive asks?
- For unwelcome news, have I selected the appropriate Buffer based on the target audience and their predicted reaction?
- Did I personalize the final output to ensure it passes the "Wade Test"?

CHAPTER 21: INTRODUCTION TO PART IV: THE CASEBOOK

In the previous chapters, we have assembled a complete toolkit for outcome-driven communication. We have the human-led strategy (Parts I-II) and the AI-powered workflow (Part III). Now, we put it all together.

This chapter provides real-world examples of common business messages, broken down by their full "Agile Message Strategy." You will see how the strategy dictates the structure, style, and stickiness, and how the AI workflow (Prompt, Refine, Personalize) executes the plan.

For the time-pressed leader, Appendix A provides the 60-second diagnostic for every message in this casebook.

Your Mission

Your mission in Part IV is not just to read these examples, but to **steal them.**

Use this Casebook as your personal template library. When you face a similar business situation, whether it's celebrating a win or delivering unwelcome news, open this section, find the matching strategy, and adapt it to your context.

Chapter 22: The Celebration (Positive Non-Persuasive) Focuses on messages with **Direct Structure** and **Rallying Cry Style.** These are pure positive messages used to build morale, share wins, and strengthen relationships without asking for anything in return. Positive messages work for all target audiences because the message is positive from the audience's point of view.

Chapter 23: The Pitch (Positive Persuasive) Focuses on messages with **Direct Structure** (often using AIDA) and **Rallying Cry Style.** These are positive, persuasive messages where you need to inspire action, getting buy-in, budget, or a partnership. Just like positive messages, positive persuasive messages work for all target audiences, because the desired outcome or action requested from the target audience has a positive impact from the audience's point of view.

Chapter 24: The Directive (Non-Sensitive) Focuses on messages with **Direct Structure** and **Clear Directive Style.** These are the workhorse messages of daily management, routine updates, instructions, and non-sensitive information where clarity is the only goal. Just like positive and positive persuasive messages, non-sensitive messages work for all target audiences, because the desired outcome or action requested from the target audience has a neutral impact from the audience's point of view. The target audience may think that this is just "business as usual."

Chapter 25: The Command (Internal Negative / Downward) Focuses on messages with **Direct Structure** and **Corporate Authority Style.** These are internal negative messages for downward communication targeting subordinates. You will learn how to deliver non-negotiable news and firm directives with absolute clarity.

Chapter 26: The Correction (Internal Negative Persuasive / Downward) Focuses on messages with **Hybrid Structure** and **Corporate**

Authority Style. These are internal negative persuasive messages for downward communication targeting subordinates. You will learn how to guide your team through difficult changes or correct performance issues while maintaining authority.

Chapter 27: The Decline (Internal Negative Non-Persuasive / Upward) Focuses on messages with **Hybrid Structure** and **Diplomatic Shield Style.** These are internal negative non-persuasive messages for upward communication targeting superiors. You will learn to say "No" firmly but politely to a boss or peer when the decision is final, non-negotiable, and persuasion is not needed.

Chapter 28: The Pivot (Internal Negative Persuasive / Upward) Focuses on messages with **Hybrid Structure** and **Diplomatic Shield Style.** These are internal negative persuasive messages for upward communication targeting superiors. You will master the high-stakes skill of delivering unwelcome news (like a delay or project failure) to your boss while persuading them to accept a new plan or direction.

Chapter 29: The Refusal (External Negative Non-Persuasive / Upward) Focuses on messages with **Indirect Structure** and **Diplomatic Shield Style.** These are external negative non-persuasive messages targeting stakeholders like customers or partners. You will learn how to deliver final decisions (like rejections) safely.

Chapter 30: The Negotiation (External Negative Persuasive / Upward) Focuses on messages with **Indirect Structure** and **Diplomatic Shield Style.** These are external negative persuasive messages. You will learn how to deliver unwelcome news (like price hikes) while persuading the client to maintain the relationship.

Chapter 31: Conclusion to Part IV We wrap up the Casebook and prepare you for the final phase: Building an Agile Culture.

The Casebook Matrix below will help you navigate. Find your intent, choose your message, and execute with confidence.

Let's open the Casebook!

The Agile Message Strategy Matrix

<table>
<tr><th>Message Type
Target Audience</th><th>Message Structure</th><th>Message Style</th><th>Stickiness Principles</th><th>Persuasiveness Principles</th></tr>
<tr><td>Positive Message
Universal Audiences</td><td rowspan="4">Direct</td><td rowspan="2">Rallying Cry</td><td rowspan="3">SUCCES</td><td>N/A</td></tr>
<tr><td>Positive Persuasive Message
Universal Audiences</td><td>Reciprocity
Social Proof</td></tr>
<tr><td>Non-sensitive Message
Universal Audiences</td><td>Clear Directive</td><td>N/A</td></tr>
<tr><td>Negative Message
Internal Stakeholders: Subordinates</td><td rowspan="2">Corporate Authority</td><td rowspan="2">Simple
Credible
Concrete</td><td>N/A</td></tr>
<tr><td>Negative Persuasive Message
Internal Stakeholders: Subordinates</td><td rowspan="3">Hybrid</td><td>Authority
Commitment</td></tr>
<tr><td>Negative Message
Internal Stakeholders: Superiors</td><td rowspan="4">Diplomatic Shield</td><td>Simple
Credible</td><td>Authority
Reciprocity</td></tr>
<tr><td>Negative Persuasive Message
Internal Stakeholders: Superiors</td><td>Simple
Credible
Concrete</td><td>N/A</td></tr>
<tr><td>Negative Message
External Stakeholders</td><td rowspan="2">Indirect</td><td>Simple
Credible</td><td>Liking
Scarcity</td></tr>
<tr><td>Negative Persuasive Message
External Stakeholders</td><td>Simple
Credible
Concrete</td><td>N/A</td></tr>
</table>

CHAPTER 22: THE CELEBRATION

Positive Non-Persuasive Messages to Receptive Universal Audiences

This chapter focuses on "Green Light" messages that require no action other than celebration or acknowledgment. The goal is to deliver a dopamine hit.

- Desired Outcome: Inspire, Validate, Build Culture
- Target Audience: Receptive universal audiences.
- Structure: Direct (BLUF)
- Style: Rallying Cry (Forceful, Personal, Colorful)
- Stickiness: Very High (9-10)

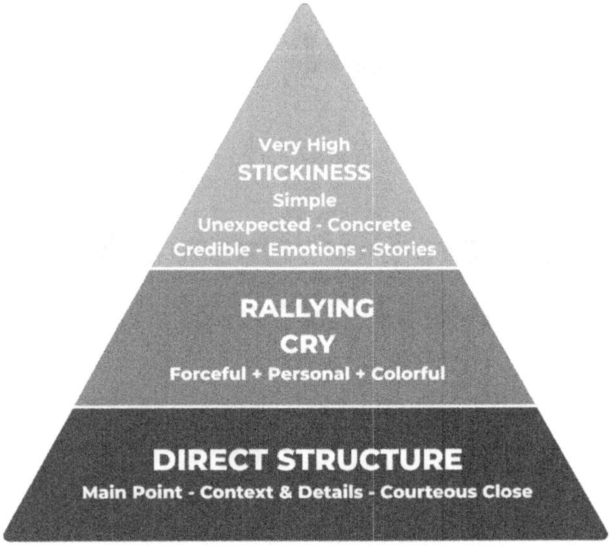

POSITIVE NON-PERSUASIVE MESSAGE
(UNIVERSAL AUDIENCES)

Case 1: The "Win" Announcement

The Agile Message Strategy

- Business Situation: Celebrating a specific team's success.
- Commander's Intent: Recognize the Q3 product launch success and publicly praise specific employees to reinforce a culture of excellence and boost team morale.
- Audience: The Product Team (High Trust).
- Message Type: Direct Structure, Rallying Cry Style, High Stickiness (Stories, Emotional).
- Channel: Email + Slack.
- Measurement: Positive replies/emoji reactions.
- Transparency: No disclosure (Personal).
- Prompt Framework: CO-STAR.

The Message

Subject: WE DID IT! Project Nova is Live!
Team, as of 9:00 AM today, Project Nova is officially live. **(Main Point)**
We didn't just hit the deadline; we crushed the quality targets. This win belongs to Sarah, who caught the critical bug last night, and David, whose design is already getting rave reviews.
Take a moment to celebrate. You earned it.
Proud to collaborate with you,
[Your Name]

Refine the Message with the Human Anchor

The Human Anchor: "Mention the 'pizza and chaos' energy of the war room and specifically thank Marcus for catching that logic error 10 minutes before the Q3 launch, proving that our grit is what won the day."

The Refined Message

Subject: WE DID IT! Project Nova is Live!
Team, as of 9:00 AM today, Project Nova is officially live. **(Main Point)**
We didn't just hit the deadline; we crushed the quality targets. This win belongs to all of you who powered through the "pizza and chaos" energy of the war room this past week.
I want to specifically thank Marcus for catching that logical error just 10 minutes before the Q3 launch. It was a heart-stopping moment, but it proved that our collective grit is what truly won the day. This success also belongs to Sarah, who caught a critical bug during the final hours, and David, whose design is already receiving rave reviews from our first users.
Take a moment to celebrate. You earned every bit of this victory.
Proud to collaborate with you,
[Your Name]

Cultural Context:

- Low Context: Specific individual praise is highly motivating.
- High Context: Focus praise on the collective group effort to avoid singling people out publicly.

Case 2: The Milestone Report

The Agile Message Strategy

- Business Situation: Sharing a major success with your boss.
- Commander's Intent: Inform leadership that the Q3 target was hit early to validate their investment in the team and build confidence for future resource requests.
- Audience: The CEO/VP (Busy).
- Message Type: Direct Structure, Rallying Cry Style (Professional yet Proud).
- Channel: Email.
- Measurement: A "Great job" reply.
- Transparency: No disclosure.
- Prompt Framework: CO-STAR.

The Message

Subject: Q3 Goal: 100% Complete (3 Weeks Early)
Hi David,
I am thrilled to report that as of today, the sales team has crossed the $1M revenue mark for Q3. **(Main Point)**
The Context: We hit this target 21 days ahead of schedule, despite the market forecasts.
The Driver: This result was driven by the new "Speed-to-Lead" protocol we implemented last month.
We are now pushing to exceed the stretch goal by end of quarter.

Cultural Context:

- Low Context: Direct credit taking ("We hit this") shows confidence.
- High Context: Share credit with the boss's guidance ("Thanks to your support, we achieved...").

Case 3: The Client Appreciation

The Agile Message Strategy

- Business Situation: Strengthening a relationship with a key partner/client.
- Commander's Intent: Thank a key client for a successful year reinforcing our partnership and set a positive tone for the renewal conversation next month.
- Audience: Strategic Client.
- Message Type: Direct Structure, Rallying Cry Style (Warm/Appreciative).
- Channel: Email (or Handwritten Note).
- Measurement: Warm reply.
- Transparency: No disclosure.
- Prompt Framework: CO-STAR.

The Message

Subject: Celebrating our 1-year anniversary
Hi Sarah,
I realized today marks exactly one year since we launched the Alpha program together. **(The Main Point)**
I just wanted to send a personal note of thanks. Your team's feedback wasn't just helpful; it was the secret ingredient that shaped our entire roadmap.
Thank you for being a true partner. Here's to another record-breaking year.

Cultural Context:

- Low Context: Short and warm is fine.
- High Context: May require more formal, elaborate language honoring the relationship and shared history.

CHAPTER 23: THE PITCH

Positive Persuasive Messages to Receptive Universal Audiences

This chapter focuses on "The Ask." You have a great idea, but you need others to act. You use high energy and clear benefits (WIIFM) to drive adoption.

- Desired Outcome: Persuade, Sell, Get a "Yes"
- Target Audience: Receptive universal audiences.
- Message Type: Positive Persuasive
- Structure: Direct (AIDA Framework)
- Style: Rallying Cry (Forceful, Personal, Colorful)
- Stickiness: High (8-10)

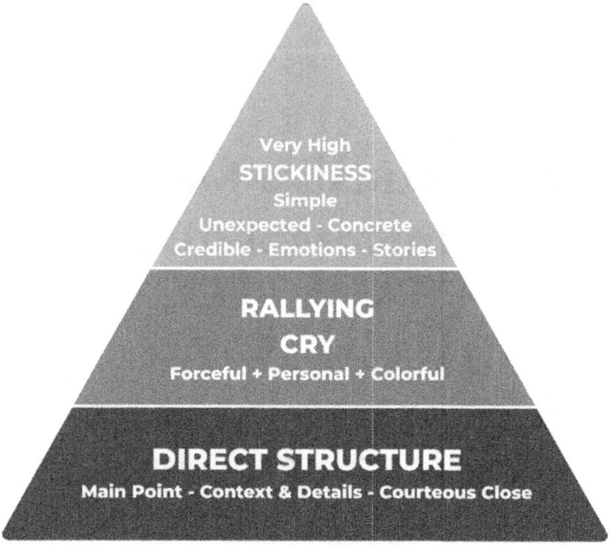

POSITIVE PERSUASIVE MESSAGE (UNIVERSAL AUDIENCES)

Case 1: The "Opt-In" Invite

The Agile Message Strategy

- Business Situation: Persuading the team to join a new initiative.
- Commander's Intent: Get the team to sign up for optional AI training to help them automate their busy work and reclaim their weekends.
- Audience: Overworked Employees.
- Message Type: Direct (AIDA), Rallying Cry Style. Stickiness (Emotional)
- Channel: Email.
- Measurement: Sign-ups.
- Transparency: No disclosure.
- Prompt Framework: CO-STAR.

The Message

Subject: A new way to master AI (and get your weekends back) **(Main Point)**
Team,
I know everyone is feeling buried in "busy work."
The Opportunity: I've found a new AI masterclass focused, specifically on our roles.
The Benefit: The goal isn't more work; it's to save you 5 hours a week by automating the boring stuff.
The Ask: This is optional, but I highly recommend it. Sign up here by Friday if you want to join the pilot group.

Cultural Context:

- Low Context: "Save time" is a strong individual motivator.
- High Context: Frame it as "Helping the team stay competitive."

Case 2: The Innovation Pitch (Internal Upward)

The Agile Message Strategy

- Business Situation: Persuading a boss to budget for a new idea.
- Commander's Intent: Secure a pilot budget for a new software tool to automate 20% of support tickets without increasing headcount.
- Audience: The CTO (Skeptical).
- Message Type: Direct (AIDA), Rallying Cry Style (Entrepreneurial). Stickiness: High (Unexpected)
- Channel: Email.
- Measurement: Meeting booked.
- Transparency: No disclosure.
- Prompt Framework: CO-STAR.

The Message

Subject: Opportunity: Cutting support costs by 20% with one tool **(Main Point)**
Hi Jen, I've found a way to automate 20% of our Tier 1 support tickets without hiring more staff.
The Insight: A new tool, 'Tool X,' creates self-service flows instantly.
The Proposal: I'm asking for a $1,000 budget to run a 30-day test. If it works, we will save 40 hours a week. If not, we learn fast and move on.
Can I get the green light to test this?

Personalize with the Human Anchor

"Reference our recent audit where we found 20% of tickets are manual repeats and frame this as the 'Entrepreneur' solution to keep headcount flat while scaling."

Cultural Context:

- Low Context: Direct pitch in the first sentence is respected.

- High Context: Use a Hybrid structure. Acknowledge current success before suggesting a new path to avoid implying the current way is "bad."

Case 3: The Strategic Alliance (External Upward)

The Agile Message Strategy

- Business Situation: Pitching a partnership to a peer organization.
- Commander's Intent: Secure a meeting with a potential partner to explore an integration that would solve a major pain point for both our user bases.
- Audience: CEO of a Partner Company.
- Message Type: Direct (AIDA), Rallying Cry Style (Visionary).
- Channel: LinkedIn / Email.
- Measurement: Meeting booked.
- Transparency: No disclosure.
- Prompt Framework: CO-STAR.

The Message

Subject: Idea: 1+1 = 3 for our customers
Hi Mark,
Your customers need better analytics. My customers need better data. **(Main Point)**
Vision: A strategic integration between our platforms would solve the #1 pain point for both our user bases instantly.
The Proposal: A 15-minute chat to see if our roadmaps align.
Are you open to a brief discussion?

Cultural Context:

- Low Context: "1+1=3" is a clear, respected hook.
- High Context: Requires a formal introduction first. Cold pitching is often ignored.

CHAPTER 24: THE DIRECTIVE

Non-Sensitive Routine Messages to Receptive Universal Audiences

These are the workhorse messages of your day. The goal is zero friction. You want the reader to understand and act instantly. This is "business as usual."

- Desired Outcome: Clarity, Efficiency, Speed
- Target Audience: Receptive universal audiences.
- Structure: Direct (BLUF)
- Style: Clear Directive (Forceful, Personal, Colorless)
- Stickiness: High (8-10)

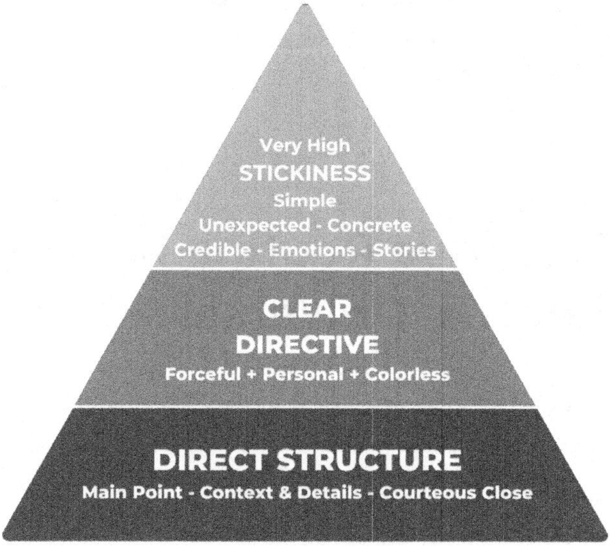

NON-SENSITIVE MESSAGE
(UNIVERSAL AUDIENCES)

Case 1: The Routine Request

The Agile Message Strategy

- Business Situation: Asking for standard approval.
- Commander's Intent: Get approval for a software renewal to ensure uninterrupted service for the sales team.
- Audience: Your Manager (Busy).
- Message Type: Direct Structure, Clear Directive Style, Stickiness: High (Simple).
- Channel: Email.
- Measurement: Approval ("Yes").
- Transparency: Low Transparency (Process).
- Prompt Framework: RTF.

The Message

Subject: Approval Needed: Salesforce Renewal ($5k) **(Main Point)**
Hi Mark,
Please approve the renewal attached for our Salesforce licenses ($5,000) so that our sales team can continue using the software service without interruptions.
Context: This is our standard annual renewal, budgeted in Q1 cost center. No changes to terms.
Link to approve: [Link]
Thanks,
[Your Name]

Cultural Context:

- Low Context: The brevity is respectful.
- High Context: Add a polite opening: "I hope you are having a good week."

Case 2: The Process Update

The Agile Message Strategy

- Business Situation: Announcing a minor operational change.
- Commander's Intent: Inform the team about a new meeting room booking system to eliminate the double-booking conflicts we faced last month.
- Audience: The Team (Neutral).
- Message Type: Direct Structure, Clear Directive Style, Low Stickiness.
- Channel: Email + Intranet.
- Measurement: Compliance (No double bookings).
- Transparency: Low Transparency (Process).
- Prompt Framework: RTF.

The Message

Subject: Process Update: New Meeting Room Booking System
Team,
Effective Monday, we are moving all room bookings to RoomFinder.
Why: To eliminate the double-booking issues, we faced last month.
Action: Please delete your recurring calendar holds and re-book them in RoomFinder by Friday.
Guide attached.

Cultural Context

- Low Context: The brevity is respectful.
- High Context: Add a positive opening: "Our sales team has been very efficient using Salesforce on a daily basis."

Case 3: The Status Report

The Agile Message Strategy

- Business Situation: Providing a standard update.
- Commander's Intent: Update leadership on the Q3 project status to confirm we are on track and flag one minor risk.
- Audience: Executive Stakeholders.
- Message Type: Direct Structure (BLUF), Clear Directive Style. Stickiness: High.
- Channel: Email.
- Measurement: No follow-up questions needed.
- Transparency: Low Transparency (Process).

The Message

Subject: Q3 Project Status: Green (On Track) **(Main Point)**
BLUF: The Q3 integration project is on schedule for the Oct 1 launch. Testing is 90% complete.
Key Updates:

- Milestone 1: Completed ahead of schedule.
- Budget: 5% under budget.
- Risk: Minor API delay from vendor (minimal impact), monitoring closely.

Full report attached.

Cultural Context

- Low Context: The brevity is respectful.
- High Context: Add a positive opening: "You approved a good project plan. We can execute it as planned."

Case 4: The Meeting Agenda

The Agile Message Strategy

- Business Situation: Setting expectations for a meeting.
- Commander's Intent: Prep the team for the strategy session so we can make a final decision on the 2026 roadmap in the room.
- Audience: Direct Reports.
- Message Type: Direct Structure, Clear Directive Style, Stickiness.
- Channel: Calendar Invite + Email.
- Measurement: Team arrives prepared.
- Transparency: Low Transparency (Process).

The Message

Subject: Agenda: 2026 Roadmap Decision
Team,
The goal of tomorrow's meeting is to finalize the 2026 roadmap. We will not be brainstorming; we will be deciding. **(Main Point)**
Prep Required: Please review the attached pre-read (3 pages) and come ready to vote on Option A vs. Option B.

Cultural Context

- Low Context: The brevity is respectful.
- High Context: Add a positive opening: "You have developed a good roadmap. The goal of tomorrow's meeting is to finalize it."

CHAPTER 25: THE COMMAND

Negative Non-Persuasive Messages to Subordinates as Audiences

These messages deliver hard news or firm rules. The goal is not to be liked; it is to be understood. Ambiguity here causes chaos.

- Desired Outcome: Compliance, Clarity, Non-Negotiable News
- Target Audience: Subordinate Annoyed Employees
- Structure: Direct (BLUF)
- Style: Corporate Authority (Forceful, Impersonal, Colorless)
- Stickiness: Average (5)

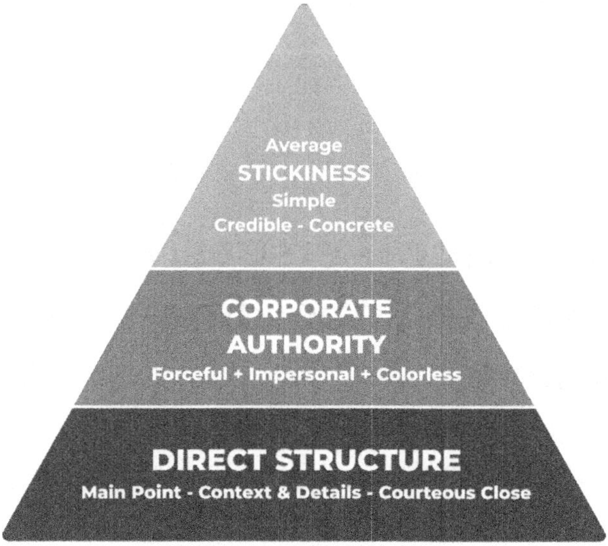

NEGATIVE NON-PERSUASIVE MESSAGE (SUBORDINATES AS AUDIENCES)

Case 1: The Policy Mandate

The Agile Message Strategy

- Business Situation: Enforcing a new, unpopular expense policy.
- Commander's Intent: Ensure 100% compliance with a new expense audit requirement to meet the mandatory standards set by our external auditors.
- Audience: Employees (Likely annoyed).
- Message Type: Direct Structure, Corporate Authority Style, Stickiness: Simple, Credible, Concrete
- Channel: Email (Official Record).
- Measurement: 100% Compliance.
- Transparency: "Drafted with AI assistance for policy accuracy."
- Prompt Framework: RTF.

The Message

Subject: POLICY UPDATE: Mandatory Receipt Uploads
Effective November 1, all expense reports must include a digital receipt uploaded to Expensify. **(Main Point)**
The Change: We can no longer accept paper receipts or emailed PDFs.
The Reason: This is a mandatory requirement from our external auditors for 2026 compliance.
Any report submitted without digital receipts after Nov 1 will be returned.

Cultural Context:

- Low Context: Direct logic ("Auditors require it") is sufficient.
- High Context: Employees may feel untrusted. Frame it as "Protecting the company together."

Case 2: The "No" to a Request

The Agile Message Strategy

- Business Situation: Firmly declined a subordinate's request.
- Commander's Intent: Decline the request for extra headcount because the Q4 budget is frozen.
- Audience: Subordinate Manager.
- Message Type: Direct Structure, Corporate Authority Style, Stickiness: Simple, Credible, Concrete
- Channel: Email (after a conversation).
- Measurement: Acceptance of the decision.
- Transparency: No disclosure.

The Message

Subject: Decision: Q4 Headcount Request
Hi Sarah,
Regarding your request for an additional junior analyst in Q4: The request is declined. **(Main Point)**
Reason: The Q4 hiring budget is frozen company-wide to meet our EOY profitability targets. We can revisit this in the Q1 planning cycle.

Cultural Context

- Low Context: The brevity is respectful, although the message is negative.
- High Context: Use Hybrid Structure: "The Q4 hiring budget is frozen company-wide to meet our EOY profitability targets, therefore the request is declined. We can revisit this in the Q1 planning cycle."

Case 3: The Immediate Correction

The Agile Message Strategy

- Business Situation: Addressing a critical safety or compliance issue.
- Commander's Intent: Stop dangerous behavior immediately to ensure physical safety in the warehouse.
- Audience: Operations Team.
- Message Type: Direct Structure, Corporate Authority Style, Stickiness: Simple, Credible, Concrete.
- Channel: SMS / PA System / Signage.
- Measurement: Immediate cessation of unsafe behavior.
- Prompt Framework: RTF.

The Message

URGENT SAFETY NOTICE:
Stop working immediately in Zone B. **(Main Point)**
A chemical spill has been detected. Evacuate to the North Parking Lot. Do not return until the "All Clear" signal is given.

Cultural Context

- Low Context: Safety first!
- High Context: Safety first!

Case 4: The Layoff Announcement

The Agile Message Strategy

- Business Situation: Communicating a restructuring decision.
- Commander's Intent: Announce the restructuring clearly so that affected employees know the next steps and remaining employees understand the future.
- Audience: Entire Company.
- Message Type: Direct Structure, Corporate Authority Style, Stickiness: Simple, Credible, Concrete.
- Channel: Live Meeting (CEO) followed by email.
- Measurement: Clarity (Reduction of rumors).

The Message (Email Follow-up)

Subject: Important Organizational Changes
Team,
Today we announced a restructuring of our operations division. **(Main Point)** This was a difficult decision made to align our workforce with our new digital first strategy.
The Impact: 15 roles in the Ops team have been eliminated. Affected employees have already been notified and offered severance packages.
Next Steps: We will hold a Town Hall at 2 PM to discuss the path forward.

Cultural Context:

- Low Context: Directness reduces anxiety for survivors.
- High Context: This Direct structure is often seen as brutal. A Hybrid structure (starting with values/regret) is essential.

CHAPTER 26: THE CORRECTION

Negative Persuasive Messages to Subordinates as Audiences

This chapter covers the delicate art of "coaching" via text. You need to change behavior without destroying motivation.

- Desired Outcome: Correct Performance, Get Buy-In
- Target Audience: Subordinate Skeptic Employees
- Structure: Hybrid (Buffer, Problem, Solution)
- Style: Corporate Authority (Forceful, Impersonal, Colorless)
- Stickiness: Average (5)

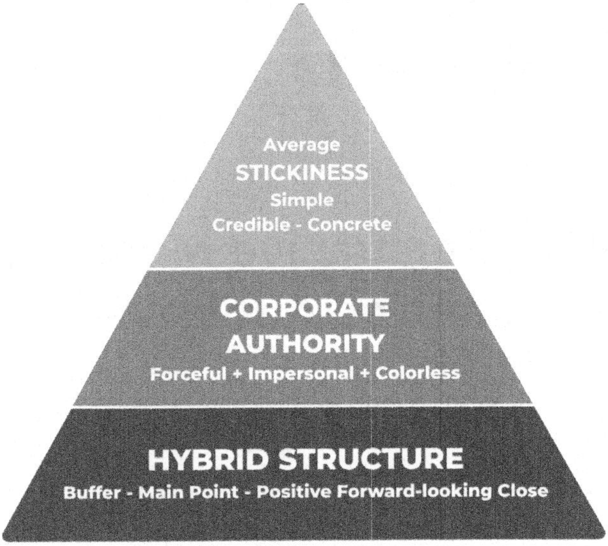

NEGATIVE PERSUASIVE MESSAGE (SUBORDINATES AS AUDIENCES)

Case 1: The Performance Correction

The Agile Message Strategy

- Business Situation: Addressing a missed deadline with a direct report.
- Commander's Intent: Correct the behavior (missed deadlines) to ensure we protect our renewal chances with the client.
- Audience: An underperforming employee (Defensive).
- Message Type: Hybrid Structure, Clear Directive Style, Stickiness: Simple, Credible, Concrete
- Channel: Email (Follow-up to meeting).
- Measurement: Behavior change (Deadlines met).
- Prompt Framework: Chain-of-Thought.

The Message

Subject: Recap: Q3 Deliverables and Timeline
Hi John,
I want to follow up on our discussion regarding the Q3 report.
The Context: As we discussed, the client deadline was yesterday, and we have not yet submitted the final draft. This puts our renewal at risk.
The Correction: Going forward, I need you to flag any potential delays 48 hours in advance. This allows us to manage client expectations proactively. **(Main Point)**
Please send me the current draft by 2:00 PM today so we can get this back on track.

Cultural Context

- Low Context: A buffer softens the blow.
- High Context: You might want to consider Indirect Structure.

Case 2: The Behavioral Adjustment

The Agile Message Strategy

- Business Situation: Addressing a cultural or behavioral issue.
- Commander's Intent: Stop the chronic lateness to meetings to respect the team's time and improve efficiency.
- Audience: A perpetually late employee.
- Message Type: Hybrid Structure, Clear Directive Style, Stickiness: Simple, Credible, Concrete
- Channel: 1:1 Meeting (Email follow-up).
- Measurement: On-time arrival.

The Message

Subject: Meeting Expectations
Hi Alex,
Context: Our daily stand-ups are designed to be short and efficient (15 mins). When you arrive 5-10 minutes late, we must restart updates, which wastes the team's time.
Expectation: Starting tomorrow, please ensure you are logged in by 9:00 AM sharp. **(Main Point)**

Cultural Context

- Low Context: A buffer softens the blow.
- High Context: You might want to consider Indirect Structure.

Case 3: The "Buy-In" for Change

The Agile Message Strategy

- Business Situation: Persuading the team to accept a difficult change.
- Commander's Intent: Get the team to adopt the new CRM to reduce their admin time eventually.
- Audience: Skeptical Sales Team.
- Message Type: Hybrid Structure (AIDA), Clear Directive Style.
- Channel: Email.
- Measurement: Adoption Rate.

The Message

Subject: Why we are switching CRMs (and how it helps you)
Team,
I know switching tools is a pain.
The Problem: We are currently losing 5 hours a week manually entering data into our old system.
The Solution: The new CRM automates that entry. It will take 2 hours to learn this week, but it will save you 200 hours next year. **(Main Point)**
Please complete the training module by Friday.

Cultural Context

- Low Context: A buffer softens the blow.
- High Context: You might want to consider Indirect Structure.

Case 4: The Project Reset

The Agile Message Strategy

- Business Situation: Realigning a team that has gone off track.
- Commander's Intent: Pause the current workstream to prevent us from building a feature the customer doesn't want.
- Audience: Project Team.
- Message Type: Hybrid Structure, Clear Directive Style, Stickiness: Simple, Credible, Concrete.
- Channel: Slack/Email.
- Measurement: Work stops/redirects.

The Message

Subject: PAUSE: Project Beta Scope
Team,
We have received new data from the beta users.
Insight: Users are not using the "Social Share" feature we are building.
The Reset: We are pausing dev on "Social Share" effective immediately. We will pivot to the "Reporting" feature instead. **(Main Point)**
Let's discuss the new sprint plan at 2 PM.

Cultural Context

- Low Context: A buffer softens the blow.
- High Context: You might want to consider Indirect Structure, if employees have put a lot of effort in developing the "Social Share" feature.

CHAPTER 27: THE DECLINE

Negative Non-Persuasive Messages to Superiors as Audiences

These are internal negative non-persuasive messages for upward communication targeting superiors. You will learn to say "No" firmly but politely to a boss or peer when the decision is final and persuasion is not the goal.

- Desired Outcome: Polite Refusal, Clarity, Relationship Preservation
- Target Audience: Disappointed Superiors or Peers
- Structure: Hybrid (Buffer, Problem, Solution)
- Style: Diplomatic Shield (Passive, Impersonal, Colorless)
- Stickiness: Average (5)

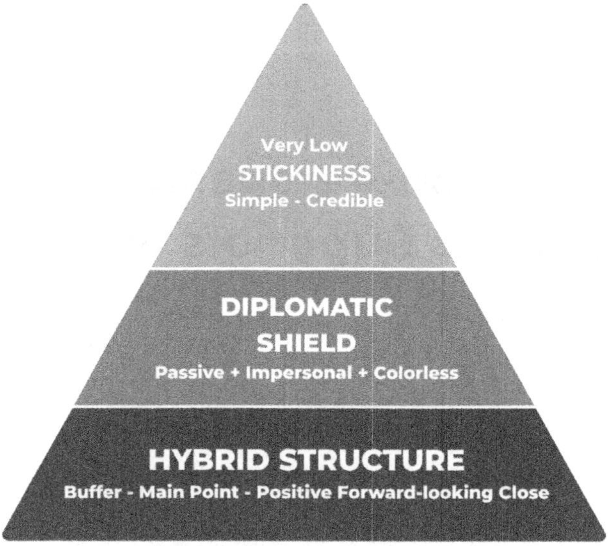

NEGATIVE NON-PERSUASIVE MESSAGE
(SUPERIORS AS AUDIENCES)

Case 1: Declining a Project Request

The Agile Message Strategy

- Business Situation: Saying no to a manager asking for resources for a new initiative.
- Commander's Intent: Decline the request to take on Project Odyssey because our team is fully committed to the Q4 roadmap and cannot take on new work without risking current deliverables.
- Audience: Your manager.
- Message Type: Hybrid Structure, Diplomatic Shield Style, Stickiness: Simple, Credible, Concrete.
- Channel: Email (after a conversation if possible).
- Measurement: Acceptance of refusal.
- Transparency: Low Transparency (Process).

The Message

Subject: Resource Allocation for Project "Odyssey"
Hi [Manager's Name],
Thanks for considering our team for Project Odyssey. We agree it's a valuable project.
The Context (Buffer): We have reviewed our current capacity against the Q4 roadmap. Our engineering team is currently 100% allocated to the critical Alpha launch deliverables.
The Challenge (Problem): Taking on Odyssey now would overextend the team and jeopardize the Alpha launch schedule.
The Decision (Solution): Therefore, we will not be able to take on Project "Odyssey" at this time. We recommend revisiting this in Q1. **(Main Point)**

Cultural Context

- Low Context: A buffer softens the blow.
- High Context: Be more formal: "Dear Mr. Manager, Thank you for

CHAPTER 28: THE PIVOT

Negative Persuasive Messages to Superiors as Audiences

These are internal negative persuasive messages for upward communication targeting superiors. You will master the high-stakes skill of delivering unwelcome news to your boss while persuading them to accept a new plan or direction.

- Desired Outcome: Deliver Bad News & Persuade on Next Steps
- Target Audience: Reluctant Superiors or Peers
- Structure: Hybrid (Buffer, Problem, Solution)
- Style: Diplomatic Shield (Passive, Impersonal, Colorless)
- Stickiness: Average (5)

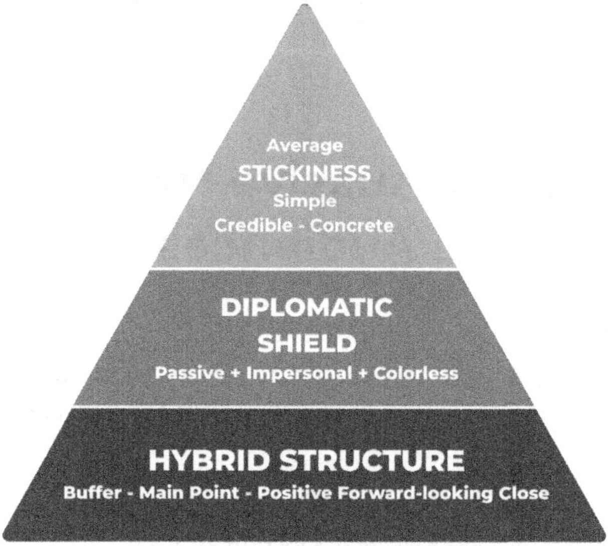

NEGATIVE PERSUASIVE MESSAGE (SUPERIORS AS AUDIENCES)

Case 1: The Delivery Delay

The Agile Message Strategy

- Business Situation: Informing a superior that a deadline will be missed.
- Commander's Intent: Inform leadership of the delay early to manage stakeholder expectations and secure approval for the recovery plan.
- Audience: VP of Engineering.
- Message Type: Hybrid Structure, Diplomatic Shield Style, Stickiness: Simple, Credible, Concrete.
- Channel: Email immediately.
- Measurement: Acceptance of new timeline.
- Transparency: Low Transparency (Process).

The Message

Subject: Request for Delay to Alpha Launch
Hi [Manager Name],
During final QA, we identified a security vulnerability in the login module.
The Impact: We cannot release the product safely until this is patched. This will require a 48-hour delay to the launch window.
Recovery: The team is working on the patch now. We expect to deploy the fix by Thursday AM and launch on Friday.

Cultural Context

- Low Context: A buffer softens the blow.
- High Context: Be more formal: "Dear Mr. Manager, … or consider the Indirect Structure.

Case 2: The Project Pivot

The Agile Message Strategy

- Business Situation: Proposing a strategic change of direction.
- Commander's Intent: Convince leadership to pivot the project strategy to align with new market data and avoid sunk costs.
- Audience: Senior Leadership Team.
- Message Type: Hybrid Structure, Diplomatic Shield Style, Average Stickiness.
- Channel: Memo / Email.
- Measurement: Approval to pivot.
- Transparency: Low Transparency (Process).

The Message

Subject: Strategic Recommendation: Project Beta Pivot
Hi [Name],
We have reviewed the initial user feedback for Project Beta.
Insight: While users love core functionality, adoption is lagging due to complexity.
The Pivot: We recommend simplifying the interface and focusing solely on the mobile experience for the next sprint. This aligns with our mobile-first strategy and addresses the primary user complaint. **(Main Point)**
We have outlined the revised roadmap in the attached document.

Cultural Context

- Low Context: A buffer softens the blow.
- High Context: Be more formal: "Dear Mr. Manager, ... or consider the Indirect Structure.

CHAPTER 29: THE REFUSAL

Negative Non-Persuasive Messages to External Audiences

These are external negative non-persuasive messages targeting stakeholders like customers or partners. You will learn how to deliver final decisions (rejections) safely.

- Desired Outcome: Safety, Reputation, Legal Protection, Closure
- Target Audience: Customers, Business Partners, or Strategic Suppliers.
- Structure: Indirect (Buffer, Rationale, Bad News)
- Style: Diplomatic Shield (Passive, Impersonal, Colorless)
- Stickiness: Very Low (2-4)

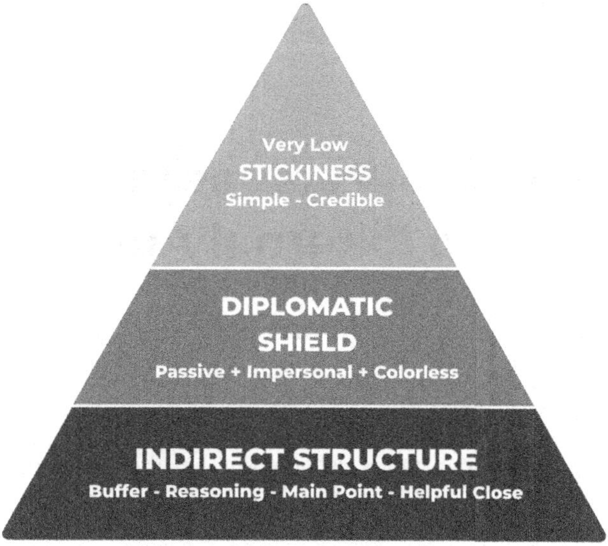

NEGATIVE NON-PERSUASIVE MESSAGE
(EXTERNAL AUDIENCES)

Case 1: The Contract Termination (External)

The Agile Message Strategy

- Business Situation: Ending a vendor relationship.
- Commander's Intent: Terminate the agreement legally to stop paying for a service that is underperforming.
- Audience: Vendor Account Manager.
- Message Type: Indirect Structure, Diplomatic Shield Style, Stickiness: Simple, Credible.
- Channel: Email (Formal Notice).
- Measurement: Confirmation of cancellation.
- Transparency: Low Transparency (Process).

The Message

Subject: Notice of Termination: Service Agreement #1234
Dear [Name],
We have been reviewing our operational costs and vendor partnerships for the upcoming fiscal year.
The Decision: Based on our changing business requirements, we have decided not to renew our contract for 2026.
Next Steps: Please consider this our formal 30-day notice. We would like to wrap up the final deliverables by [Date].

Cultural Context

- Low Context: A buffer softens the blow.
- High Context: Consider sending a letter.

Case 2: The Rejection

The Agile Message Strategy

- Business Situation: Rejecting a job candidate.
- Commander's Intent: Provide a final "No" to close the hiring process with zero legal risk.
- Audience: Job Applicant.
- Message Type: Hybrid Structure, Diplomatic Shield Style, Stickiness: Simple, Credible.
- Channel: Email.
- Measurement: No reply.

The Message

Subject: Your Application for Senior Manager
Dear [Name],
Thank you for the time you spent interviewing with our team.
We have completed our review process and have decided to move forward with another candidate for this position.
We wish you the best in your job search.

Cultural Context

- Low Context: A buffer softens the blow.
- High Context: Consider sending a letter.

CHAPTER 30: THE NEGOTIATION

Negative Persuasive Messages to External Audiences

This covers unwelcome news where you do want to keep the relationship (e.g., price hikes, pushing back on scope).

- Desired Outcome: Deliver Bad News & Retain Relationship
- Target Audience: Reluctant Customers, Business Partners, and Suppliers
- Structure: Indirect (Buffer, Rationale, Bad News, Close)
- Style: Diplomatic Shield (Passive, Impersonal, Colorless)
- Stickiness: Average (6)

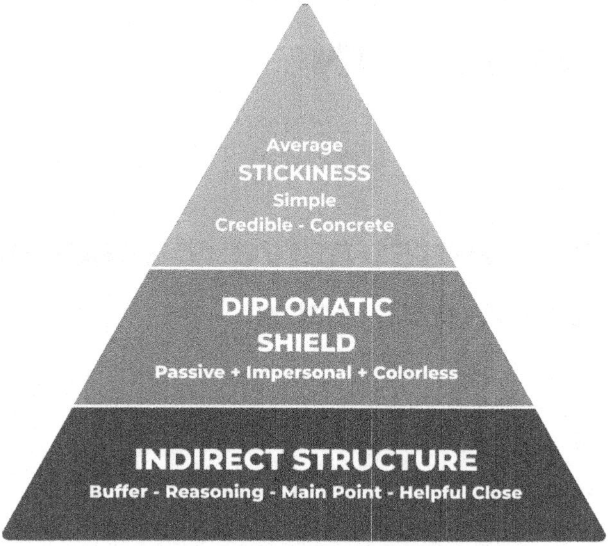

NEGATIVE PERSUASIVE MESSAGE (EXTERNAL AUDIENCES)

Case 1: The Client Pushback

The Agile Message Strategy

- Business Situation: Refusing a client's request for out-of-scope work.
- Commander's Intent: Refuse the extra work to protect the launch deadline while keeping the client happy.
- Audience: A demanding Client.
- Message Type: Indirect Structure, Diplomatic Shield Style, Stickiness: Simple, Credible, Concrete.
- Channel: Email.
- Measurement: Client accepts "No" but stays on board.

The Message

Subject: Re: Request for additional feature set
Hi Sarah,
Thank you for sending over the ideas for the new reporting module. We agree these features would add value.
The Constraint: Currently, the engineering team is fully allocated to delivering the Core 2.0 launch by your October deadline. Adding scope now would jeopardize that date.
The Decision: We will not be able to include these features in the current sprint. However, we have added them to the backlog for Q1 review. **(Main Point)**

Cultural Context

- Low Context: Personal touch "Hi, Sarah, ..." softens the blow.
- High Context: Be more formal: Dear Ms. Sarah …

Case 2: The Price Increase

The Agile Message Strategy

- Business Situation: Informing customers of higher costs.
- Commander's Intent: Announce a price hike while persuading customers that the new value justifies the cost.
- Audience: Demanding customers.
- Message Type: Indirect Structure (AIDA), Diplomatic Shield Style, Stickiness: Simple, Credible, Concrete.
- Channel: Email.
- Measurement: Low Churn rate.

The Message

Subject: Update to your subscription pricing
Dear Customer,
For the past three years, we have been committed to providing you with the most reliable hosting service on the market.
The Context: To maintain that level of quality and security in a changing market, we are updating our pricing structure.
The Change: Effective Jan 1, your monthly subscription will adjust to $29/mo.
The Value: This change allows us to continue investing in the 24/7 support and security upgrades you rely on.

Cultural Context

- Low Context: Personal touch "Hi, Sarah, ..." softens the blow.
- High Context: Be more formal: Dear Ms. Sarah …

CHAPTER 31: CONCLUSION TO PART IV

You now have a library of core templates covering the full spectrum of leadership communication.

You have seen how the **Strategy** (Intent/Audience) dictates the **Structure** (Direct/Hybrid/Indirect) and the **Style** (Rallying Cry/Clear Directive/Corporate Authority/Diplomatic Shield). And how the **Stickiness** principles (Simple, Unexpected, Credible, Concrete, Emotional, and Stories) can be used to make your message stick, make them memorable, if needed.

These templates are your starting point. But remember the final rule of the Agile Workflow: **Personalize.** Use these structures, but fill them with your voice, your data, and your specific context.

You are now ready for the final phase of your journey: Moving from an Agile Communicator to an Agile Organization.

Turn the page to the Conclusion: **Building an Agile Culture.**

CHAPTER 32: CONCLUSION: BUILDING AN AGILE CULTURE

You have now mastered the system. We began this journey with a simple but powerful premise: **Strategy First, AI Second** Now, at the end, that principle has been transformed into a complete, actionable framework.

You have the human-led wisdom to define the Message Strategy. You have the technical skill to command the AI Workflow. You have moved from being a reactive writer to an initiative-taking Pilot. But personal mastery is only the first step.

THE BOTTOM LINE

The goal of this framework is not just to save you time, it is to change how your organization thinks. Reclaiming 1,200 hours allows you to move from **Management** (pushing paper) to **Leadership** (shaping strategy and people).

KEY TAKEAWAYS

The Monday Morning Protocol Agile leadership starts with setting new standards. Re-allocate your reclaimed time into three imperatives:

- Strategy: Thinking on business, not just in it.
- People: Mentoring leaders and building "relationship capital."
- Customers: Engaging directly with those you serve.

Becoming the Editor-in-Chief To transform your culture, you must mandate the standards you've learned:

- Share the Unbreakable Rule: Stop writer-centric behavior.
- Deploy Traffic Light: Use shared language for message structure.
- Crowdsource your Style Guide: Collaboratively ban jargon to create a unified, authentic brand voice.

THE FINAL VERDICT

In the age of AI, the ability to generate text is free. The ability to generate **clarity** is priceless. The future will be won by the most trusted humans, those who use technology to amplify their humanity, not replace it.

Part 1: The Dividend (What to Do with 1,200 Hours)

We calculated that leaders lose 1,200 hours a year to inefficient communication. By mastering this framework, you are reclaiming that time. But saving time is not the goal; reallocating it is.

Don't just use this time to answer more emails. Invest it in the strategic imperatives that only a human leader can execute:

- **Strategy:** The time to think, reflect, and work on the business, not just in it.
- **People:** The time to mentor your leaders and build the relationships that are the true glue of the organization.
- **Customers:** The time to leave the "bubble" of headquarters and engage directly with the people you serve.

Part 2: The Action Plan (The Monday Morning Protocol)

Agile leaders don't just communicate better; they build a culture where everyone communicates better. If you are the only one using "Bottom Line Up Front" (BLUF) while your team is still sending you walls of text, you will still drown in noise.

Your final mission is to become the Editor-in-Chief of your organization. Start this transformation on Monday:

- **Share the "Unbreakable Rule":** Forward Chapter 2 to your direct reports. Tell them: "From now on, every email must be written for the reader, not the writer."
- **Mandate the "BLUF":** Set a new standard for your team updates. "If I can't find the main point in the first two sentences, I will send it back unread."
- **Deploy the "Traffic Light":** Use the language of Structure. When you assign a sensitive task, say: "This is a Red-Light message. Use the Indirect Structure."
- **Crowdsource Your Style Guide:** Don't write a rulebook from the top down. Ask your team to build a "Banned Jargon" list (e.g., "synergies," "leverage") together. This creates buy-in for your new voice.

Part 3: The Theory (Fulfilling the Manifesto)

As you execute this protocol, remember that you are fulfilling the core values of the Agile Manifesto we adapted in Chapter 6:

- **Message Outcomes over Comprehensive Prose:** You are prioritizing clarity and results over length.
- **Audience Collaboration over One-Way Broadcasting:** You are analyzing your audiences emotions, showing empathy, and respecting their feedback over shouting orders at them.
- **Human Strategy over Automated Tools:** You are using AI as an assistant, never as a replacement for your judgment.

- **Responding to Feedback over Following a Script:** You are using the OODA loop to adapt your message in real-time.

The Future of Leadership

In the age of AI, the ability to generate text is free. The ability to generate clarity is priceless. The future of communication will not be won by the best AI; it will be won by the most trusted humans. It will be won by the leaders who can cut through the noise, align their teams with a single sentence, and use technology to amplify their humanity, not replace it.

You have the controls. The flight plan is filed. Go lead.

ACKNOWLEDGEMENTS

My professional journey has been shaped by the support of many organizations and individuals. I thank my former employers and colleagues at Ekokem Corporation, Padaeng Industry (PDI) Public Company Limited (PCL), and Aneo Software Oy, as well as the foreign chambers of commerce in Thailand. These organizations provided me with a global arena to hone my strategic messaging and communications skills.

I am deeply grateful to Aalto University Executive Education (Aalto EE) and the Aalto Executive MBA Program (2013–2014). Earning this certificate, granted by the Aalto University School of Business, provided the strategic framework necessary to navigate today's disruptive business environment. The program's emphasis on inventive strategies, AI-enabled transformation, and the dialogue between sustainability and radical creativity was instrumental in renewing my professional perspective.

A special note of thanks goes to Professor Dr. Ronald E. Dulek, the John R. Miller Professor of Management at the University of Alabama, whose guidance as visiting professor of the Aalto Executive MBA Program in 2014 was invaluable. He showed me how to choose the best message structure, style, and stickiness for any business situation. He has co-authored books called: Bottom Line Business Writing, The Business Writing Style Book, and Strategic

Messaging which I have used as reference guides for my business writing over the years.

I am also profoundly grateful to Ben Nothnagel, Senior Advisor at Aalto EE. His expertise in emotional intelligence and self-development deepened my understanding of high-performance leadership, specifically how it effectively balances empathy and authority, and provided critical insights into the link between personal wellbeing and organizational results.

I owe a debt of gratitude to my cross-cultural cohort in the Aalto Executive MBA Program. Our collaborative team assignments were a profound learning ground, revealing the nuances of cultural context in corporate communications and teaching me how to navigate diverse perspectives effectively.

I acknowledge the Thai Institute of Directors (Thai IOD) Association and my fellow cohort members from the Director Certification Program (DCP 266). Completing the program in 2018 and becoming a Fellow Member marked a significant milestone in my corporate governance journey. This experience highlighted the critical nature of the CEO-Chairman-Board interface, underscoring that effective board communications are a strategic imperative for defining vision, ensuring robust risk oversight, and navigating complex legal environments.

Finally, I thank my wife, Angsumarin, who is the love of my life. She has been my bridge between worlds, helping me deeply understand the beliefs, values, and cultural nuances that distinguish the East from the West.

APPENDIX A: THE AGILE COMMUNICATOR'S CHEAT SHEET

THE MESSAGE STRATEGY

Why am I writing? (Commander's Intent)

- **Desired Outcome:** What specific action must my reader take?
- **Strategic Intent:** Why is it important?

Who am I writing for? (Audience Analysis)

- **Trust Level:** High, low, or new?
- **Hierarchy:** Upward, downward, or lateral?
- **Cultural Context:** High (indirect) or Low (direct)?
- **Predicted Reaction:** Pleased, Skeptical, or Displeased?

What do they care about? (WIIFM)

- **People think:** "What's in it for me?"

How will it be delivered? (The Channels)

- Email (paper trail), IM (speed), or meeting (nuance)?

How will I measure success? (The Measurement)

- Hard Metric: (e.g., Did they click the link? Did support tickets decrease?)
- Soft Metric: (e.g., Was the reply tone less hostile? Did I get invited to the next meeting?)

By answering these five questions the Leader can write the Agile Message Strategy and hand it out to the Analyst, Researcher, Writer, and Editor.

THE MESSAGE TYPE

The Structure (The "Bones" of the Message)

- **Direct (Green Light):** Main point first. Use for good or neutral news.
- **Hybrid (Yellow Light):** Buffer/Problem first. Use for persuasive or sensitive news.
- **Indirect (Red Light):** Buffer/Rationale first. Use for bad news to a displeased audience.

The Stickiness Level (The "Soul" of the Message)

- **Very High (8–10):** (Inspire/Persuade) Use all SUCCES principles.
- **Average (5–6):** (Comply/Consider) Use Simple, Concrete, Credible.
- **Very Low (2–4):** (Clarity/Finality) Use Simplicity and Credibility.

The Style (The "Voice" of the Message)

- **The Rallying Cry:** (Forceful + Personal + Colorful) Use to inspire and motivate.
- **The Clear Directive:** (Forceful + Personal + Colorless) Use for daily management and tasks.
- **The Diplomatic Shield:** (Passive + Impersonal + Colorless) Use for sensitive news, de-escalation, and high-context situations.
- **The Corporate Authority:** (Forceful + Impersonal + Colorless) Use for formal, non-negotiable policies.

The Analyst reads the Agile Message Strategy, analyzes the target audience, and selects the best Message Type that will most likely produce the desired outcome.

The Researcher reads the Agile Message Strategy, brainstorms ideas and collects information and data for the Writer

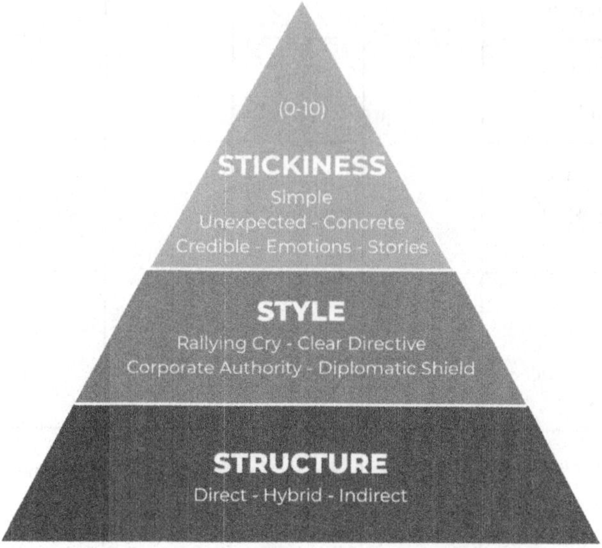

THE AGILE MESSAGE STRATEGY

THE AGILE MESSAGE STRATEGY MATRIX

<table>
<tr><th>Message Type
Target Audience</th><th>Message
Structure</th><th>Message
Style</th><th>Stickiness
Principles</th><th>Persuasiveness
Principles</th></tr>
<tr><td>Positive Message
Universal Audiences</td><td rowspan="4">Direct</td><td rowspan="2">Rallying Cry</td><td rowspan="3">SUCCES</td><td>N/A</td></tr>
<tr><td>Positive Persuasive Message
Universal Audiences</td><td>Reciprocity
Social Proof</td></tr>
<tr><td>Non-sensitive Message
Universal Audiences</td><td>Clear Directive</td><td>N/A</td></tr>
<tr><td>Negative Message
Internal Stakeholders: Subordinates</td><td rowspan="2">Corporate Authority</td><td rowspan="2">Simple
Credible
Concrete</td><td>N/A</td></tr>
<tr><td>Negative Persuasive Message
Internal Stakeholders: Subordinates</td><td rowspan="3">Hybrid</td><td>Authority
Commitment</td></tr>
<tr><td>Negative Message
Internal Stakeholders: Superiors</td><td rowspan="4">Diplomatic Shield</td><td>Simple
Credible</td><td>Authority
Reciprocity</td></tr>
<tr><td>Negative Persuasive Message
Internal Stakeholders: Superiors</td><td>Simple
Credible
Concrete</td><td>N/A</td></tr>
<tr><td>Negative Message
External Stakeholders</td><td rowspan="2">Indirect</td><td>Simple
Credible</td><td>Liking
Scarcity</td></tr>
<tr><td>Negative Persuasive Message
External Stakeholders</td><td>Simple
Credible
Concrete</td><td>N/A</td></tr>
</table>

THE CORE AI WORKFLOW

The Leader defines the Commander's Intent; The Analyst analyzes the target audience, predicts the audience's reaction, and selects the message type. The Researcher gathers information and data.

- MESSAGE STRATEGY (The Leader): Define Commander's Intent.
- MESSAGE TYPE (The Analyst): Select the Message Type.
- MESSAGE DETAILS (The Researcher): Gathers information and data.
- **PROMPT (The Writer):** Translate your strategy into an expert prompt for your AI Assistant. Use the frameworks to write your prompts: CO-STAR (Context, Objective, Style, Tone, Action, Response), RTF (Role, Task, Format), or AIM (Actor, Input, Mission)
- **REFINE (The Editor):** Iterate with your AI Assistant. Check for accuracy, tone, and concision. Ask for variations.
- **PERSONALIZE (The Leader):** This is the non-negotiable human step. Add your authentic voice, context, and empathy to build trust.

The Writer reads the Agile Message Strategy and uses the collected information and data to write the first draft or the prompt for the AI Assistant who writes the first draft,

The Editor reads the Agile Message Strategy and refines the first draft by evaluating and iterating the message with the AI Assistant.

The Leader receives the refined message and personalizes the message, if needed. The Leader can ask the AI Assistant to evaluate the final message so that the Leader can fine tune the message, if needed, before sending it to the audience.

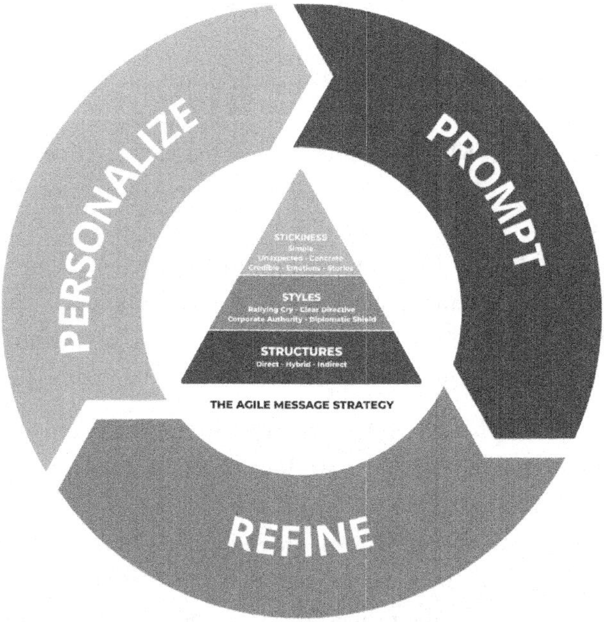

THE CORE AI WORKFLOW

APPENDIX SUPPLEMENT: THE PERSUASION MATRIX

Based on the foundational persuasion principles defined by Robert Cialdini in *Influence: The Psychology of Persuasion*, this matrix provides the "invisible levers" needed to elevate your writing.

You can use these principles across the four persuasive message types to make the "agile move" that answers your reader's unspoken needs and drives measurable business results:

- Positive persuasive messages targeting universal audiences.
- Negative persuasive messages targeting internal audiences (subordinates).
- Negative persuasive messages targeting internal audiences (superiors).
- Negative persuasive messages targeting external audiences.

The Principles of Persuasion

Here are the six persuasion principles and how to use them in messaging:

Reciprocity: Give Before You Ask The human brain is wired to return favors. In business writing, offer value upfront to create a psychological "indebtedness."

- The Agile Move: Provide a useful template, a white paper, or a specific insight before your Call to Action.
- AI Prompt Tip: "Rewrite this sales email to lead with a valuable industry insight rather than a request for a meeting."

Commitment & Consistency: Leverage Small Wins People strive to align their current actions with past commitments.

- The Agile Move: Start with a "micro-commitment," such as asking for a newsletter sign-up or a simple "yes" to a non-controversial question.

- AI Prompt Tip: "Structure this pitch to lead with three easy-to-agree-upon facts about our industry's current challenges."

Social Proof: Use the Power of the Crowd In uncertainty, people look to others. Use testimonials, data points, and "The Crowd" to build credibility.

- The Agile Move: Use specific numbers ("95% of our users...") rather than vague claims ("Most of our users...").
- AI Prompt Tip: "Insert three placeholder slots for specific customer metrics that demonstrate social proof."

Liking: Humanize the Pilot We are more likely to say "yes" to people we like. Authenticity is the antidote to synthetic text.

- The Agile Move: Use conversational language and find common ground. Share a brief "Proof of Life" story.
- AI Prompt Tip: "Function as an Editor. Make this report sound more approachable and human while maintaining executive authority."

Authority: Cite the Masters People defer to expertise. Establish your authority (and your AI Assistant's) by citing data and frameworks.

- The Agile Move: Cite industry research or established models (like the SUCCES model).
- AI Prompt Tip: "Ground this recommendation in the latest McKinsey research on digital transformation."

Scarcity: Create an Urgent Knowledge Gap We value what is rare. Create a sense of urgency without sounding like a used-car salesman.

- The Agile Move: Highlight time-sensitive opportunities or exclusive "Pilot Group" access.
- AI Prompt Tip: "Refine this invitation to emphasize that the beta-testing window closes this Friday." For a deep dive into the theory and AI prompts for these levers, refer to Chapter 10: The Psychology of Influence.

Principle	When to Use	The Agile Move (The "Now What?")
Reciprocity	Lead Generation / Sales	Offer a high-value template or insight before you ask for a meeting.
Commitment	Change Management	Secure a small "Yes" (e.g., newsletter sign-up) to build a path toward a larger mandate.
Social Proof	Building Trust	Use hard metrics ("95% success rate") rather than vague adjectives ("excellent results").
Liking	Relationship Building	Share a brief personal "Proof of Life" story to humanize the digital void.
Authority	Strategy Approval	Ground your claims in established frameworks like the OODA Loop or SUCCES model.
Scarcity	Driving Urgency	Highlight the "Knowledge Gap" or time-sensitive nature of the opportunity.

THE PREFLIGHT CHECKLIST

Do not proceed until you can check these four boxes:

I – The Co-Pilot Selection

- Have you chosen your specific AI Assistant for your role?
- Do you have the enterprise version to protect your data?

II – The Prompt Engineering

- Do you have the CO-STAR and RTF frameworks saved somewhere accessible?
- Are you ready to stop typing "write an email" and start typing strategic instructions?

III – The AI Workflow

- Have you committed Step Zero?
- Will you refuse to open the chatbot until you have defined your message strategy?

IV – The Transparency Policy

- Have you sent the Team Policy to your direct reports?
- Does everyone know the "rules of the road?"

THE FINAL CHECKLIST

I – The Commander's Intent

- Strategic Intent: Why is the message important?
- Desired Outcome: What is the required action?

II – The Analyst's Blueprint

- Target Audience: What is the predicted reaction?
- Communication Channel: What is the main channel?
- Document Type: What is the document type?
- Structure: What is the structure: Direct, Indirect, or Hybrid?
- Style: What is the style: Rallying Cry, Clear Directive, Corporate Authority, or Diplomatic Shield?

III – The Writer's Craft

- Stickiness: What stickiness principles are in use: Simple, Unexpected, Credible, Concrete, Emotional, or Stories?
- Persuasiveness: What persuasion principles are in use: Reciprocity, Commitment, Social Proof, Liking, Authority, or Scarcity?

IV – The Final Verification

- AI Verification: Did we run the Accuracy, Tone, and Strategy passes?
- Proof of Life: Is my unique human voice present in the first and last lines?
- Transparency: Should I disclose AI use: Yes / No?

Final Question: Should I send it, refine it, or delete it?

SOURCES

- This list includes works that are directly cited, quoted, or referenced in the text of Messaging Made Agile.

- Amber Case. "How small memos can make large organizational changes | by Amber Case - Medium," accessed November 16, 2025.
- Anthropic. 2025. "Claude 3.7 Sonnet: Controlled Reasoning and Extended Thinking for High-Stakes Decisions." Anthropic AI Blog. February 2025. https://www.anthropic.com/news/claude-3-7-sonnet.
- Atlassian. "How to deliver difficult news with compassion to your employees...," accessed November 16, 2025.
- BCCampus. "1.4 Case Study: The Cost of Poor Communication - Technical Writing Essentials," accessed November 16, 2025.
- Beck, Kent, et al. "Manifesto for Agile Software Development." AgileManifesto.org, 2001.
- Bernoff, Josh. Writing Without Bullshit: Boost Your Career by Saying What You Mean. HarperBusiness, 2016.
- BetterUp. "The Minto Pyramid Principle Explained (With Example Frameworks)," accessed November 16, 2025.
- Brown, Brené. Dare to Lead: Brave Work. Tough Conversations. Whole Hearts. Random House, 2018. (Referenced for change management synthesis).

- Cialdini, Robert B. Influence: The Psychology of Persuasion. Revised Edition. Harper Business, 2006.
- Coram, Robert. Boyd: The Fighter Pilot Who Changed the Art of War. Little, Brown and Company, 2002.
- DeepSeek-AI. 2025. "DeepSeek-R1: Incentivizing Reasoning Capability in LLMs via Reinforcement Learning." arXiv preprint. January 2025. https://arxiv.org/abs/2501.12948.
- Dhawan, Erica. "When to Use Which Communication Channel." Harvard Business Review, October 19, 2023.
- Dulek, Ronald E., Chad B. Hilton, and Kim Sydow Campbell. Strategic Messaging. Pearson Custom Publishing, 2003.
- Ettore, Michael L. "Commander's Intent Defined." Marine Corps Gazette (April 1993).
- Fielden, John S., and Ronald E. Dulek. Bottom-Line Business Writing. Prentice Hall, 1984.
- Garner, Bryan A. Garner's Modern English Usage. 4th ed., Oxford University Press, 2016.
- GovTech Singapore. 2024. "The CO-STAR Framework: A High-Performance Blueprint for Prompt Engineering." Data Science & AI Division. https://www.gov.sg/article/the-costar-framework.
- Grammarly. "State of Business Communication: The Backbone of Business Is Broken." Grammarly & The Harris Poll, 2022.
- Grossman, David. "Define the 'Outcome' as 1st Step to Effective Communication." The Grossman Group blog, May 22, 2020.
- Hall, Edward T. Beyond Culture. Anchor Books, 1976.
- Heath, Chip, and Dan Heath. Made to Stick: Why Some Ideas Survive and Others Die. Random House, 2007.
- Kotter, John P. Leading Change. Harvard Business Review Press, 2012. (Referenced for change management framework).
- Max, Tucker. "The One Unbreakable Rule in Business Writing." Harvard Business Review, September 13, 2016.
- Miller, Donald. Building a StoryBrand: Clarify Your Message So Customers Will Listen. HarperCollins Leadership, 2017.
- Minto, Barbara. The Minto Pyramid Principle: Logic in Writing, Thinking and Problem Solving. Minto International, 1987.

- Moffatt v. Air Canada, 2024 BCCRT 149 (Civil Resolution Tribunal, British Columbia, Can).
- Munoz, Oscar. United Airlines 2017 Crisis Response Memo. (Case study on empathetic failure).
- Nadella, Satya. Hit Refresh: The Quest to Rediscover Microsoft's Soul and Imagine a Better Future for Everyone. Harper Business, 2017. (Referenced for Growth Mindset).
- O'Hair, Dan, Friedrich, Gustav W. and Dixon, Lynda Dee. “Strategic Communication in Business and the Professions.” Pearson, 2015.
- OpenAI. 2025. "OpenAI o3: Frontier Reasoning and Advanced Chain-of-Thought Capabilities." OpenAI Technical Report. https://openai.com/index/o3-report/
- Pixar Animation Studios. The Braintrust Methodology. (Referenced as a model for innovation).
- Porter, Michael E., and Nitin Nohria. "How CEOs Manage Time." Harvard Business Review, July–August 2018.
- Pozen, Robert C., Aleksandra (Saška) Mojsilović, and Angelina G. Wang. "How AI-Generated Communication Shapes Perceptions of Leaders." Harvard Business Review, March 27, 2024.
- Silverman, David. "Why Is Business Writing So Bad?" Harvard Business Review, February 2009.
- Takeuchi, Hirotaka, and Ikujiro Nonaka. "The New New Product Development Game." Harvard Business Review, Jan 1986.
- Wiens, Kyle. "I Won't Hire People Who Use Poor Grammar. Here's Why." Harvard Business Review, July 20, 2012.
- Wiens, Kyle. "Why Everyone Is a Writer in an Agile Culture." Harvard Business Review, February 26, 2015.

FURTHER READING

This list includes supplemental resources for readers who wish to explore related topics in greater depth.

- Agility PR Solutions. "Bad connection: Study finds poor communication costs businesses ...," accessed November 16, 2025, https://www.agilitypr.com/pr-news/pr-skills-profession/bad-connection-study-finds-poor-communication-costs-businesses-1-2-trillion-annually/
- Aisha Babangida. "Building Business Acumen Through Emotional Intelligence," accessed November 16, 2025.
- Ann Handley. "10 Ways to Create a Writing Culture - Ann Handley," accessed November 16, 2025.
- Ariel Group. "Accessed November 16, 2025," https://www.arielgroup.com/three-ways-to-more-efficient-team-business-writing/
- Aroscop. "How Purpose-Led Brands Can Connect with their Audience - Aroscop," accessed November 16, 2025, https://www.aroscop.com/how-purpose-led-brands-can-connect-with-their-audience/
- backstitch. "AI in Workplace Communications: Pros, Cons and Tips," accessed November 16, 2025.

- BDC. "10 tips for effective business writing - BDC," accessed November 16, 2025, https://www.bdc.ca/en/articles-tools/entrepreneurial-skills/become-better-communicator/10-tips-effective-business-writing
- Benjamin Ball Associates. "10 Common Business Writing Mistakes - Avoid Writing Errors - Benjamin Ball Associates," accessed November 16, 2025, https://benjaminball.com/blog/common-business-writing-mistakes/
- Benjamin Ball Associates. "BLUF, AIM, AIDA: 17 Powerful Presentation Frameworks Guide - Benjamin Ball Associates," accessed November 16, 2025, https://benjaminball.com/blog/guide-to-powerful-presentation-frameworks/
- Blink. "The ultimate internal communication style guide | Blink," accessed November 16, 2025.
- Boyd, Robert. Boyd: The Fighter Pilot Who Changed the Art of War.
- Coursera. "7 Ways to Improve Your Writing Skills - Coursera," accessed November 16, 2025, https://www.coursera.org/articles/writing-skills
- Classy Writing. "5 Ways to Write with Empathy in Business," accessed November 16, 2025.
- Communication Skills Academy. "Why your team NEEDS a writing style guide," accessed November 16, 2025.
- Digitaloft. "13 Copywriting Frameworks You Need to Know - Digitaloft," accessed November 16, 2025, https://digitaloft.co.uk/copywriting-frameworks/
- Duarte Inc. "HBR Guide to Persuasive Presentations - Duarte Inc.," accessed November 16, 2025,
- https://www.duarte.com/resources/books/hbr-guide-to-persuasive-presentations/
- Farmer School of Business. "Six Cs of Business Communication - Farmer School of Business," accessed November 16, 2025, http://www.fsb.miamioh.edu/fsb/content/programs/howe-writing-initiative/HWI-handout-CsofBusComm.html

- Fleximize. "Adapting Communication Styles to Different Audiences - Fleximize," accessed November 16, 2025, https://fleximize.com/articles/000592/communication-styles
- Fleximize. "A Simple Guide to Writing in Plain English - Fleximize," accessed November 16, 2025, https://fleximize.com/articles/409363/writing-in-plain-english
- FluentCRM. "9+ Awfully Bad Email Examples You Must Not Send [and How to Fix Them] - FluentCRM," accessed November 16, 2025, https://fluentcrm.com/bad-email-examples/
- Forbes Vetted. "Best AI Writing Tools 2025 - Forbes Vetted," accessed November 16, 2025, https://www.forbes.com/sites/forbes-personal-shopper/article/best-ai-writing-tools/
- Garner, Bryan. Garner's Modern English Usage.
- GCFGlobal.org. "Business Communication: How to Write a Clear Business Memo," accessed November 16, 2025, https://edu.gcfglobal.org/en/business-communication/how-to-write-a-clear-business-memo/1/
- GetGenie Ai. "7 Best Copywriting Frameworks with Example for Better Conversions - GetGenie Ai," accessed November 16, 2025, https://getgenie.ai/best-copywriting-frameworks/
- Google Books. "HBR Guide to Persuasive Presentations - Nancy Duarte - Google Books," accessed November 16, 2025, https://www.google.com/search?q=https://books.google.com/books/about/HBR_Guide_to_Persuasive_Presentations.html%3Fid%3DOzuGcOYix3EC
- Gregory Ciotti. "To Create a Culture of Writing at Your Company, Start by Providing Incentive | by Gregory Ciotti | ThinkGrowth.org," accessed November 16, 2025, https://thinkgrowth.org/to-create-a-culture-of-writing-at-your-company-start-by-providing-incentive-c393e777d80f
- Hamel, Gary, and C.K. Prahalad. "Strategic Intent." Harvard Business Review, May–June 1989.
- Hurley Write. "4 Ways to Improve Your Team's Professional Writing Skills Fast," accessed November 16, 2025, https://www.hurleywrite.com/4-ways-improve-team-writing-fast/

- Hurley Write. "Analyze Your Audience for Better Professional Writing - Hurley Write," accessed November 16, 2025, https://www.hurleywrite.com/analyzing-your-audience-in-professional-writing/
- Hurley Write. "Examples of Bad Emails (and What They Reveal About Poor Writing)," accessed November 16, 2025, https://www.hurleywrite.com/examples-of-bad-emails-and-what-they-reveal/
- Kickresume. "Office Jargon Can Cost You Time ... And $6 Million a Year!" accessed November 16, 2025.
- LivePlan. "The Pros and Cons of Using AI for Business Planning | LivePlan," accessed November 16, 2025, https://www.liveplan.com/blog/planning/the-pros-and-cons-of-using-ai-for-business-planning
- Madrigal Communications. "Recognise the 12 signs of bad writing - Madrigal Communications," accessed November 16, 2025, https://madrigal.com.au/twelve-signs-of-bad-writing/
- MailMaestro. "How to Rewrite Emails with AI for Clarity & Impact - MailMaestro," accessed November 16, 2025, https://www.maestrolabs.com/how-to/rewrite-emails-with-ai
- MasterWriter. "The Pros And Cons Of AI Writing Tools - MasterWriter," accessed November 16, 2025, https://masterwriter.com/the-pros-and-cons-of-ai-writing-tools/
- Miller, Donald. Building a StoryBrand.
- Nicole Bean. "The Audience-Centric Approach: 8 Reasons Why It Matters in ...," accessed November 16, 2025, https://articlesbynicolebean.medium.com/the-audience-centric-approach-8-reasons-why-it-matters-in-marketing-9af3876fcfa4
- Onside Content. "Why Every Brand Needs an Audience Centric/Data Driven Content Strategy and What Happens Without One," accessed November 16, 2025, https://onsidecontent.com/why-every-brand-needs-an-audience-centric-data-driven-content-strategy-and-what-happens-without-one/
- Preply. "7 hidden business costs of language gaps and poor communication - Preply," accessed November 16, 2025,

https://preply.com/en/blog/hidden-business-costs-of-language-gaps-and-poor-communication/

- Priya Chaney. "Mastering Communication with the Minto Pyramid | by Priya Chaney - Medium," accessed November 16, 2025, https://medium.com/@priya.chaney/mastering-communication-with-the-minto-pyramid-271de5aef97c
- Professional Academy. "The 7 Cs of Communication | Professional Academy," accessed November 16, 2025, https://www.professionalacademy.com/blogs/the-7-cs-of-communication/
- Pumble. "Workplace Communication Statistics (2025) - Pumble," accessed November 16, 2025, https://pumble.com/learn/communication/communication-statistics/
- Purdue OWL. "Tone in Business Writing - Purdue OWL," accessed November 16, 2025, https://owl.purdue.edu/owl/subject_specific_writing/professional_technical_writing/tone_in_business_writing.html
- Rcademy. "Building Rapport and Trust through Effective Communication [9 Ways] - Rcademy," accessed November 16, 2025, https://rcademy.com/building-rapport-and-trust-through-effective-communication/
- ResearchGate. "(PDF) An Overview of Business Writing: Challenges and Solutions - ResearchGate," accessed November 16, 2025, https://www.researchgate.net/publication/333165745_An_Overview_of_Business_Writing_Challenges_and_Solutions
- Revolution Learning and Development Ltd. "The 7 Cs of Communication - Revolution Learning and Development Ltd," accessed November 16, 2025, https://www.revolutionlearning.co.uk/article/the-7-cs-of-communication/
- Scribbr. "Free AI Writing Resources | Scribbr," accessed November 16, 2025, https://www.scribbr.com/ai-writing/
- Skills You Need. "Building Rapport - Effective Communication | Skills You Need," accessed November 16, 2025, https://www.skillsyouneed.com/ips/rapport.html

- SME Strategy. "7 Methods for Leaders to Improve Their Writing Skills - SME Strategy," accessed November 16, 2025, https://www.smestrategy.net/blog/7methodsforleaderstoimprovetheirwriting
- Sparkle.io. "7 Bad Email Examples and How to Avoid Them (2025) - Sparkle.io," accessed November 16, 2025, https://sparkle.io/blog/bad-email-examples/
- Super Copy Editors. "How to Write a Business Memo in 2025 - Expert Advice - Super Copy Editors," accessed November 16, 2025, https://supercopyeditors.com/blog/writing/effective-business-memo/
- Supliful. "Examples of Poorly Written Business Emails: How to Avoid Common ...," accessed November 16, 2025, https://supliful.com/blog/examples-of-poorly-written-business-emails
- The Brief Lab. "The 3 Cs of Communication: Clear, Concise, Consistent | The Brief Lab," accessed November 16, 2025, https://thebrieflab.com/blog/the-3-cs-of-communication-clear-concise-consistent/
- The Write Direction. "5 Common Business Writing Errors to Avoid | The Write Direction," accessed November 16, 2025, https://www.thewrite-direction.com/blog/common-business-writing-errors/
- Trinka. "Trinka: AI Writing and Grammar Checker Tool," accessed November 16, 2025, https://www.trinka.ai/
- University of Colorado. "Examples of Writing Samples Before and After Plain Language | University of Colorado," accessed November 16, 2025, https://www.cu.edu/coleman/examples-writing-samples-and-after-plain-language
- University of Pittsburgh. "Audience Analysis | Department of Communication - University of Pittsburgh," accessed November 16, 2025, https://www.comm.pitt.edu/oral-comm-lab/audience-analysis
- Untools. "Minto Pyramid - Untools," accessed November 16, 2025, https://untools.co/minto-pyramid/
- USC. "4 Research Methods for Audience Analysis | University of Southern...," accessed November 16, 2025,

https://communicationmgmt.usc.edu/blog/4-research-methods-for-audience-analysis

- WildFig Marketing. "Pros and Cons of Using AI to Write Content [+ 5 Ways to Use It Effectively]," accessed November 16, 2025, https://www.wildfigmarketing.com/blog/pros-and-cons-of-using-ai-to-write-content
- Yomu AI. "The Pros and Cons of Using an AI Writing Assistant for Content Creation - Yomu AI," accessed November 16, 2025, https://www.yomu.ai/resources/the-pros-and-cons-of-using-an-ai-writing-assistant-for-content-creation
- Zapier. "The 6 best grammar checkers in 2025 - Zapier," accessed November 16, 2025, https://zapier.com/blog/best-ai-grammar-checker-rewording-tool/
- ZOKRI. "The True Cost of Poor Communication in Business," accessed November 16, 2025.

INDEX

M

N

O

P

T

V

W

ABOUT THE AUTHOR

Jorma Manninen is the founder of Business Made Agile and a subject matter expert on strategic messaging and management communication in the age of AI. For over 30 years, Jorma has worked with board members, CEOs, senior executives, and top-tier managers helping them communicate better.

Jorma is on a mission to stop unclear messaging and eliminate the billion-dollar drain of "Workslop". He believes that in the new era, your human authority and authenticity are your only true competitive advantages. He doesn't just show you how to write; he coaches you how to use Artificial Intelligence (AI) to read and write better and more quickly and how to become an Agile Communicator.

His "Strategy First. AI Second" framework, detailed in this guide, is a proven system that integrates timeless human-led strategy with the accelerating power of AI.

Jorma built the "Strategy First" principles during his 30-year business career, complementing his practical experience by studying strategic messaging and management communication under Professor Ronald E. Dulek at Aalto University's Executive MBA Program in 2013 - 2014.

An active practitioner of his "AI Second" principles, he has been an advanced user of generative AI since its public release in November 2022. His firsthand experience includes building practical workflows for Google's

Gemini and NotebookLM as well as Canva's Magic Studio, and other leading platforms he has used to write, edit, and illustrate this book.

Jorma authored this book to give business leaders a practical, step-by-step playbook, to stop unclear messaging, eliminate Workslop, and build an agile communication culture that helps build the complete agile culture.

Learn more or connect with Jorma on LinkedIn:
https://www.linkedin.com/in/jormamanninen/

BUSINESS MADE AGILE

WWW.BUSINESSMADEAGILE.COM

ABOUT THE PUBLISHER

Business Made Agile Oy is a strategic advisory firm dedicated to helping leaders navigate the intersection of modern technology and human-centric strategy. Through the Business Made Agile series, we provide frameworks for iterative growth in an AI-driven world.

Visit us at https://www.businessmadeagile.com/ to download free resources, templates, and the strategic briefing including executive summary and action roadmap of this book.

Made in United States
North Haven, CT
30 January 2026

87645591R00163